INVENTIONS
THAT
BUILT
THE
INFORMATION
TECHNOLOGY
REVOLUTION

Rhys McCarney, Ph. D.

CONTENTS

TABLE OF FIGURES

CHAPTER

1

Introduction

Receiving a windfall is a life changing experience. This event has the capacity for immensely positive or negative change. Quite often there is a mixture of both. It's an event for which one might hope and pray, and to which one may devote dreams and fantasies. Paradoxically, one is never prepared for it. It comes as a surprise.

I am a physicist with a career that dates back almost as far as the development of the integrated circuit, and I have brushed against the high tech business world many times. I've personally observed several high tech fortunes that were made as well as many attempts that failed. But most of these were in the software arena. Myself, I never set out to make money. Like many idealistic young scientists, my goal was to change the world by doing great science.

My story is rather unusual because my windfall came from hardware, not software. Laboratories, corporations and universities have built up a thick web of safety nets to prevent individual inventors from retaining rights to their intellectual property. While the inventor may receive a payment for a portion of the patent rights, in all cases the basic intellectual property (IP) rights are held by institutions. Portfolios of patents are built and institutions negotiate permissions and licenses without any interference from individual inventors. It was highly unusual that my inventions slipped through the cracks. Actually, it's more accurate to say that the relevant players were so sure that all the doors were wedged shut that they, in fact, didn't see the few open cracks.

I earned my doctorate from an Ivy League school during the recession of the 1980s. The job market was tight and I spent a few years doing postdoctoral research that was paid by fellowships that ran a year at a time. My break came when the most prestigious corporate lab in the US, which I'll call Swell Labs for the purpose of this book, lost a few staff scientists because they left for university positions. A friend of mine from graduate school was working there. He telephoned me as soon as Swell made the internal announcement that they were a few heads below their allotment and would start recruitment for two staff level positions. I sent him my resume and publication list by Fed Ex. I flew to New Jersey for an interview a week later and had an offer two days after that. Working for Swell was my dream come true. My dream job lasted a bit less than four years. Swell shut down their physical sciences research lab. The scientists could resign or they could accept a *Reduction in Force* (RIF) action. Actually, all the major corporate labs closed their basic research facilities around the same time. The more senior scientists were given six to twelve months advance notice of their termination date. I got a pink slip with 60 days notice. I packed up my lab. After separation I started looking for another job. In my spare time I started writing patent disclosures and applications.

When my windfall came, the events were rapid but not sudden. I had developed my patent portfolio over the course of 14 years. In the fall of 2005, after many years of speculation and broken time lines, a high tech company brought a product to market. It is likely that the product infringed on some of my patents. That company was not interested in my portfolio, but other companies in the same technological area began to show interest. Of greater importance, in 2004 a small company began to bring interference suits against several large corporations for a different product that was in a closely related area. The IP held by that company had some conflicts with patents in my portfolio. When this became known, interest in my portfolio escalated. It would be several years before I learned the source of the sudden significance of my IP.

I wasn't doing this all by myself. I had managed to attract the interest of two very good patent lawyers. They were sufficiently interested in my research and my IP that they worked on commission. Philip had been a partner at a large firm in Silicon Valley before starting his own practice. Nigel had worked for Philip for about five years and later would start his own practice. Philip had many contacts in the high tech community. Looking back, building and marketing my portfolio of patents was a great adventure in my life and Philip and Nigel were my partners.

All the high tech companies ignored my portfolio for years. Philip would drop hints and make calls and no one cared. But then he got a call in fall of 2006. A big high tech company, named BigTech for the purpose of this book, had vetted my patents. They had vetted me as well. They had an agenda and my IP fit in. They took the lead and things moved fairly rapidly. Of course it was Philip and Nigel who were negotiating but I never sensed that much drama. Actually, it was all rather surreal to me. There was an opening round of price negotiations. During the second round we settled on a price in the low 8 figures. Then there were some details to fulfill. It would be several months before the check arrived and reality began to sink in. My IP portfolio was a project on the side. In my day job I held a senior position at a large laboratory and made a salary that put me at the top of the middle class or in the lower part of the upper middle class (definitions vary). I had 2 kids to raise, but I could spend $5 or $10 without thinking about it too much. When the windfall came, my partners received 48% of the sale price. Fifty-two percent of a very large check is a lot of money. I paid a lot of taxes and still had more money than I'd ever expected. It truly changed my life. I can confidently state: money is great. Life is so much easier when you have money. I really, really, really recommend it.

The world financial crisis arrived shortly after my windfall. My parents had never had much money. Watching banks fail caused me to worry. They had seen banks fail in the Great Depression and those memories remained fresh for them 50 years later. I kept working my job until the crisis eased. Then my oldest child graduated from university and I only had tuition bills for one. So I retired.

For the twenty years before I retired I wondered why Swell Labs and all the other corporate labs – the best labs in the world – shut down basic research in physical science. I also wondered why there were so many large fortunes that relied entirely on the internet and/or telecommunications. After I retired, I started doing some research. A few ideas emerged. Things began to make sense. That was the motivation for starting this book. Along the way, it became evident that the structure of patent law and the business strategies associated with intellectual property were responsible for the shape of the evolution of the high technology business sector. The information technology industry comprises business, social and entertainment networks, and the hardware (computers) and software that supports it all. Information technology was an entirely negligible part of the economy five decades ago.

As I learned more I began to see a truly remarkable history. In 1975 there were a couple thousand physicists doing research in the areas of optics and semiconductor devices. Research led to a small number of inventions that were profound. These formed the technological basis for modern computers, mobile devices, the internet and broadband communication. They enabled the information technology revolution. There were a few dozen scientists who were key inventors of these innovations. At this same time, software was almost nonexistent. There were a few hundred computer scientists writing software for main frame computers. Bill Gates and Paul Allen had just started MicroSoft in the Spring of that year. There were only a few hundred people writing software for personal computers. Some 40 years later, there are roughly 5 or 6 thousand physicists doing research in the areas of optics and semiconductor devices. There are about 2 million people (in the US) writing and developing software – and each earns as much as a physicist. The five largest US technology companies (Apple, Facebook, Google, Microsoft and Amazon) are all in the software/internet/social media sector and make up 12% of the entire US market capitalization of publicly held companies (2017). Software alone provides 7% of the USGDP.

Most of the scientist inventors received letters or plaques that acknowledged the brilliance of their work. A very small number leveraged their inventions through the private sector to reach some financial success, achieving wealth on the order of $1B. A number of leaders in software (including social media and internet applications) have amassed fortunes on the order of $100B, and there are scores who have wealth on the order of $10B. In the history of private enterprise, has there ever been an occasion when so many have derived so much wealth from the inventions of so few who received so little? A small group of very smart people contributed revolutionary inventions. These people made very little profit on their work, but an entirely different group of people made vast fortunes.

After a brief introduction, this book starts with some insights about the process of invention and the structure and practice of intellectual property law. The next focus is the physical platform (hardware) that supports information technology (dominantly software). The platform is based on three main inventions, along with a few minor ones. Each was developed, in the 1960s and 70s, through the work of two or three or four key individuals. You won't recognize their names. The physical platform was in place by the early 1990s. Each of the three inventions was so successful that the platform hasn't needed any new invention for the last 25 years, and it won't need any new inventions for another 20 years to come. The next subject is the development of software as a business and a discussion of how young software companies overtook the established hardware business. Some perspective is provided by a discussion of previous technologies and earlier fortunes that were made. Finally, some implications for current and future research and development are presented.

The information technology revolution has been a world-changing event of historic proportions. Numerous software and information network entrepreneurs have made very large fortunes. The magnitude of any one of these is not unprecedented in history. But the magnitude of the net sum of the wealth is remarkable and unprecedented.

So, how did all this happen?

CHAPTER

2

Guess the Wealthy Ones

In American society, money is valued above anything else. It is not literally true to say that "money is everything," but that statement is approximately correct. People are valued according to their status, and their status is determined primarily from their net worth, or their apparent net worth.

It follows that most people in America seek to gain wealth. How does one do it? The most prevalent way to gain wealth is to inherit it. Unfortunately, inheritance is not an efficient way to become wealthy and then stay wealthy. According to a study reported in June 2015,[1] about 70% of families who attain wealth lose their wealth by the second generation. Remarkably, 90% of wealthy families lose it by the third generation. There are psychologists who study this phenomenon. They call it "sudden wealth syndrome".[2] The basic observation is that heirs and lottery winners alike have a profound tendency to blow their windfall. For example, it takes an average of 19 days for the recipient of an inheritance to buy a new car. It's possible that wealthy children feel entitled and are emotionally unprepared to manage great wealth. The reality is probably simpler and, when it comes to managing money, wealthy children are no different from anyone else. Wealth changes people. It's human nature. It tends to corrupt the soul, but that's just my opinion.

The world of business offers the best way to build wealth. Someone who is savvy, hard nosed and works hard can rise to a high position and accumulate great wealth. It helps if you like to dismember kittens and immolate puppies. But those proclivities don't set you apart from other professions such as law and science. There have been times in American history when entrepreneurship linked with invention was a path to wealth. Thomas Edison is a favorite example. Henry Ford is another example. He started out working at one of Edison's companies, then saved enough money to strike off on his own. How has high tech entrepreneurship fared in the recent past?

This book is about science, technology, invention and money in America, especially during the last four decades. To introduce the interplay between these terms, I've made up a game for you to play and it's presented in Table 1. How many names in the list in the Table do you recognize? Match the names in the left column with a contribution to modern information technology from the column in the middle. Finally, guess the person's approximate net worth (as of early 2017 if alive, otherwise at time of death) by choosing a net worth figure from the column at right. An estimate of "< $5M" is used for those cases where data are not publicly available and the net worth is assumed to be relatively small.

Table I

1) M. M. (John) Atalla	A) co-inventor of the internet (DARPA)	a) < $5M
2) Robert I. Hall	B) co-inventor of fiber optic wire (Corning Labs)	b) < $5M
3) Jack Kilby	C) co-inventor of MOSFET (Bell Labs), elemental device of digital semi-conductor technology	c) < $5M
4) Robert Kahn	D) co-founder, Google	d) < $5M
5) Paul Allen	E) co-inventor of integrated circuit (Texas Instruments)	e) < $5M
6) Larry Page	F) founder of Snapchat	f) < $5M
7) Donald Keck	G) Co-inventor of semi-conductor laser (GE Labs)	g) $100M
8) Evan Spiegel	H) principal founder of Facebook, social media	h) < $5M
9) Vinton Cerf	I) co-founder of Microsoft; computer operating systems, software	i) < $5M
10) Robert D. Maurer	J) founder of Twitter	j) < $5M
11) Jack Dorsey	K) founder of PayPal, internet shopping; also Tesla, electric autos	k) $50B

Table 1
Contributors to modern information technology are listed in
the first column. The contributions are in the middle column.
Approximate values of the fortunes of the contributors are in the right
column. Match each name with a contribution and a fortune.

Table I (cont.)

12) Larry Ellison	L) co-inventor of integrated circuit (Fairchild Semi-conductor, Intel)	l) $2.1B
13) J. Jim Hsieh	M) founder of Napster, co-counder of Facebook	m) $80B
14) Sergey Brin	N) founder of Amazon, internet shopping	n) $15B
15) Sean Parker	O) inventor of Global Positioning System - GPS (US Navy Labs)	o) $50B
16) Dawon Kahng	P) co-founder, Google	p) $2.5B
17) Bill Gates	Q) founder of Oracle, software	q) $80B
18) Jeff Bezos	R) co-inventor of fiber optic wire (Corning Labs)	r) $4B
19) Elon Musk	S) co-inventor of MOSFET (Bell Labs) Co-inventor of floating gate memory, aka FLASH memory	s) $50B
20) Roger Easton	T) co-inventor of the internet (Stanford, DARPA)	t) $35B
21) Mark Zuckerberg	U) co-inventor of semi-conductor laser (Lincoln Lab, MIT)	u) $35B
22) Robert Noyce	V) co-founder of Microsoft; computer operating systems, software	v) $1.4B

Contributors to modern information technology, continued.

How did you do? The answers are given on the next couple of pages. Look at the list and think about it for a few minutes. You probably recognize many names associated with recent contributions, but not so many from dates more than fifteen years ago.

What conclusions might one reach by thinking about this list? For one, there's a chronological correlation: those who worked in the middle to late middle of the 20th century generally did not achieve great wealth, whereas those who worked in the last two or three decades did pretty well. Another correlation involves the type of industry – hardware or software. Those who made physical inventions (hardware) that became the physical platform for communications and information processing did not become very wealthy. The most notable exception on the list is Robert Noyce. Noyce was one of the founders of Intel. On the merits of his success, he rose through the ranks at Intel and accumulated larger portions of stock in the company, and eventually reached a high position. Another exception is Jim Hsieh, a co-inventor of the diode laser. He started a company and made some money. On the other hand, those whose creations involve software have made a lot of money. Lots and lots of money. I note that software would not exist were it not for the physical communications and information processing platform that others invented and developed.

The next few chapters describe some insights about inventors, the process of invention, and some relevant issues associated with intellectual property law. If you prefer, you can skip ahead to Chapter 7 which begins the discussion of some key technologies and how some of the fortunes in Table 1 were made.

Table I Answers

1) M. M. (John) Atalla	C) co-inventor of MOSFET (Bell Labs), elemental device of digital semi-conductor technology	e) < $5M
2) Robert I. Hall	G) co-inventor of semi-conductor laser (GE Labs)	b) < $5M
3) Jack Kilby	E) co-inventor of integrated circuit (Texas Instruments)	a) < $5M
4) Robert Kahn	A) co-inventor of the internet (DARPA)	f) < $5M
5) Paul Allen	V) co-founder of Microsoft; computer operating systems, software	m) $80B
6) Larry Page	P) co-founder, Google	u) $35B
7) Donald Keck	R) co-inventor of fiber optic wire (Corning Labs)	j) < $5M
8) Evan Spiegel	F) founder of Snapchat	l) $2.1B
9) Vinton Cerf	T) co-inventor of the internet (Stanford, DARPA)	i) < $5M
10) Robert D. Maurer	B) co-inventor of fiber optic wire (Corning Labs)	d) < $5M
11) Jack Dorsey	J) founder of Twitter	v) $1.4B

Answers to the quiz presented in Table 1.

Table I Answers (cont.)

12) Larry Ellison	Q) founder of Oracle, software	o) $50B
13) J. Jim Hsieh	U) co-inventor of semi-conductor laser (Lincoln Lab, MIT)	g) $100M
14) Sergey Brin	D) co-founder, Google	t) $35B
15) Sean Parker	M) founder of Napster, co-counder of Facebook	p) $2.5B
16) Dawon Kahng	S) co-inventor of MOSFET (Bell Labs) co-inventor of floating gate memory, aka FLASH memory	c) < $5M
17) Bill Gates	I) co-founder of Microsoft; computer operating systems, software	q) $80B
18) Jeff Bezos	N) founder of Amazon, internet shopping	s) $50B
19) Elon Musk	K) founder of PayPal, internet shopping; also Tesla, electric autos	n) $15B
20) Roger Easton	O) inventor of Global Positioning System - GPS (US Navy Labs)	h) < $5M
21) Mark Zuckerberg	H) principal founder of Facebook, social media	k) $50B
22) Robert Noyce	L) co-inventor of integrated circuit (Fairchild Semi-conductor, Intel)	r) $4B

Answers to the quiz, continued.

ANSWERS:

1) C e
2) G b
3) E a
4) A f
5) V m
6) P u
7) R j
8) F l
9) T i
10) B d
11) J v
12) Q o
13) U g
14) D t
15) M p
16) S c
17) I q
18) N s
19) K n
20) O h
21) H k
22) L r

Estimates of net worth are approximate and were made in early 2017. In many cases, two or more sources offered different estimates and an average value was used.

CHAPTER

3

Intellectual Property

History has recorded many technological revolutions with impact that literally changed the world. More than any other, the development of the information technology revolution has been shaped by the nature of patent law and the business strategies that developed as a result of the law. It helps to understand a little about inventors, the process of invention and the tactics and strategies of patent law.

Everyone who flirts with being an inventor has a variation of the same dream. It starts with an idea. After a little while, there is a realization that it's a good idea. This is followed by the thought that maybe no one else has had the same idea. Almost unrelated to this thought train, the idea pops up that I might be able to make money from this idea.

If the flirtation goes further, the story follows a fairly regular pattern.[1] Each of the following steps is accompanied by an emotional roller coaster. I investigate the patent process. The process is something that an individual inventor can do. But it's expensive and it takes a long time. To start, I make written records of all the details of my idea. Then I build a simple prototype. I might build it in my garage, which is why people who flirt with inventions are called *garage inventors*. The excitement starts to build when the prototype works.

All the articles I read about the patent process tell me that I must use a patent attorney. After some false starts, I get a few recommendations and find a patent attorney I think is trustworthy. He's very reassuring, but he reminds me that it's expensive and it takes a long time.[2] He let's me help him with a patent search. Thirty years ago, patent records were bound in volumes as hard copies. A few libraries around the country held copies of these records along with indexes and cross-indexes. Many of these libraries were in Silicon Valley. In the last twenty years, the library of patents has been digitized and has become available through on-line access. A typical search involves the use of one or more appropriate key words. Every time I do a search that finds a related patent, my heart beats faster. Maybe this inventor has beaten me to the idea. I retrieve the patent and read it. Most of the time it's obvious that it's not really the same as my idea. There are times when I have an idea and I find a prior patent (a prior patent, article or other related prior publication is known as *prior art*) that in fact is rather similar. A process then follows during which I digest the prior patent and analyze the similarities and differences in a report that makes specific references to figures and lines of text.

But the former case is more common; the prior patents I find are not really very similar to my idea. I make a list of all the prior patents for my attorney, and he makes his own search. I draw up a set of notes in which I describe my idea in great detail, using figures to help the discussion. I might include descriptions of a prototype I built along with test results. My patent attorney uses my input to write a rough draft of the body of the application, the *specification*.

I read his first draft and make some remarks. We go back and forth with edits and revisions. A final version is ready after a few weeks. As the last step, my attorney writes the most important section, the *claims*. The backbone of the claims is made up of independent claims. These stake out the ideas in the most basic and broad terms. Each independent claim is followed by a series of dependent claims. These claims are narrower and describe specific aspects in greater detail. If an interference case should arise, there is a danger that the US Patent and

Trademark Office (PTO), or a court, will rule that an independent claim is too general. A dependent claim that hits the mark is difficult to dismiss. As an example, suppose I write a patent for a pair of pants that can be converted from full-length slacks to shorts. The independent claim states that each of the two legs of the pants can be attached to, or detached from, the shorts at a position near the knee. A dependent claim states that the form of attachment is a zipper. A second dependent claim states that the form of attachment is a set of snaps. A third dependent claim states that the form of attachment is Velcro. A fourth dependent claim states that the shorts and detachable legs are made from the same cut of cloth.[3]

The day my application is submitted is filled with relief. I'm sure the patent will be awarded. I'm sure my patent will bring me success. I also get a bill from my attorney and the bill includes the filing fee.

A year goes by, maybe more. I get an email from my patent attorney. In the old days, I would get a letter or phone call. He tells me that he's received the "first action" from the US Patent and Trade Office (USPTO). Several claims in my application have been allowed. However, my three independent claims have been rejected because of prior art. We have 90 days to file a rebuttal, and he suggests that we meet to discuss our response.

The day my rebuttal is submitted is filled with relief. I'm almost sure the patent will be awarded. I'm sure my patent will bring me success.

A few months go by. My patent attorney sends me an email. The Examiner has accepted our argument and has allowed all the claims. This is an extraordinary moment. I'm filled with optimism and relief. The PTO sends my attorney a Notice of Allowance. I print it out and pin it on my bulletin board.

All inventors who reach this point now have the same dream. It's a dream about money. The dream goes like this. There is an Intellectual Property (IP) office at Any Big Company (ABC). Several patent attorneys scan the records of new patents, looking to see what ideas are relevant to ABC's business interests. One of these attorneys sees my patent. He reads it carefully, especially the Claims. He brings it to the attention of the head of the IP office. The head attorney says it will be noted and he will await further developments.

Months later, the R&D department at ABC is making big strides on their next killer product (NKP). The head of R&D has a monthly meeting with IP. At the meeting, the head of IP remembers my patent and shows a copy to the head of R&D. His brows furrow as he reads it. At least two of my independent claims are directly related to the development of the NKP. He doesn't believe the product can be completed without infringing on these claims. Another meeting is called and several attorneys and engineers attend.

A few weeks later, I get an email from my patent attorney. An attorney from ABC contacted him about my invention. My attorney wants to set up a conference call with the attorney at ABC. The ABC attorney is very polite. He compliments me on my ideas and congratulates me on my patent. He asks if I can come to Los Angeles for a meeting with the Vice President of ABC to talk about terms for licensing my patent.

Well, that dream is over the top. It's really too far-fetched. Here's a more realistic version. The researchers at ABC discover that a team at Really Big Competitor (RBC) is working on something that's almost exactly like the NKP. They might come to market sooner. The head of the Research and Development (R&D) department has a monthly meeting with IP. At the meeting, the head of IP remembers my patent and shows a copy to the head of R&D. His eyes light up as he reads it. One of my independent claims and several of my dependent claims are very similar to techniques that both ABC and RBC are using. Both ABC and RBC have patents related to the product, but licensing my patents will give ABC a real advantage; RBC can't possibly proceed without infringing. A few weeks later, I get an email from my attorney. He sets up a conference call with an attorney at ABC. The ABC attorney is very polite. He compliments me on my ideas and congratulates me on my patent. He asks if I can come to Los Angeles for a meeting with the Vice President of ABC to negotiate royalties licensing my patent. All my expenses will be paid. Of course I can bring my attorney, and his expenses will be paid.

This is exactly the way it all works….. if you live in a Walt Disney dream. And perhaps it works like that in Fantasy Land at Disney World. But you can't actually live in Fantasy Land. I've looked, and there are no condominiums there. You can visit, but at the end of the day you have to leave.

The real world, of course, is nothing like that. Intellectual Property is business, and business has no rules about right or wrong or fair play. I don't think it has any rules at all, for that matter. There are no rules of fair play in Nature. A predator hunts and eats prey. There are no feelings except hunger. A businessman is the same. He has no feelings except hunger. Hunger for a profit.

And so it is with IP. The attorneys at ABC know the simple realities of IP. Infringement cannot be stopped without litigation. Litigation costs money. The financial resources of ABC are infinite compared with the resources of any individual inventor. Therefore, any individual inventor stands no chance in a lawsuit (but see below). Therefore, there is no inhibition about infringement. Attorneys at ABC do not bother to scan the listings of newly issued patents. Except in cases where they are trolling to look for ideas to steal.

Patent license fees are paid…. in the movies and other works of fiction. In real life, royalties are never paid.[4] The number of royalty contracts in force is very close to zero. Money never changes hands. The attorneys at ABC assemble a large patent portfolio and so do the attorneys at RBC. The attorneys at International Big Company (IBC) also have a huge portfolio. The attorneys at these companies get together and write agreements to trade licensing rights. Sometimes the trades involve other considerations besides patents. Never does money actually change hands.[4] Nowhere does an individual inventor fit into this scheme. Each of these companies has an R&D department. The purpose of the department is to come up with inventions that are relevant to the company, and then develop the invention into a product. Every stage in this process is tracked by the IP office and patent portfolios are developed along with the products. Any device, creation or innovation that was not born in the company R&D department bears the label "not invented here (NIH)." The company will not get involved with anything that is NIH because the IP is not "clean." The company will only pursue inventions from their own R&D department. The company controls all the IP for these inventions. Of course, that doesn't mean the company pays no attention to an important NIH invention. They will simply create an identical "invention" and claim it as their own.

How do small companies figure into this? Not at all. They are mostly ignored, or threatened and bullied if they become a nuisance. How does an individual inventor fit into all this? He or she is much less than a small company. An individual inventor is ignored. In the rare event that ignoring the inventor doesn't work, he or she is crushed. An individual inventor is nothing. The corporate labs run right over him/ her like a bug and there isn't even a dirty spot left on the windshield.

So here's how patents really work. Owning a patent means very little in the real world. It means that an Examiner at the US Patent and Trademarks Office reviewed your application, reviewed related patents, and decided that your application includes some ideas that are new. But why should ABM, or any company, recognize your intellectual property? If they ignore you, what will you do about it? How will you enforce your patent? You can bring a lawsuit. But you won't stand a chance of winning. ABM has a crew of expensive lawyers. They will hire "expert witnesses," most of whom will say whatever they are paid to say. They can say that your ideas are really the same as some ideas that were published in an obscure article three years earlier. This would put your ideas "in the public domain" and therefore not patentable. They will say the Examiner didn't have enough time to devote to the application and didn't find this reference. More likely, the ABM lawyers will make the legal proceedings as lengthy and complicated as possible. You will be forced to hire lawyers. Unless your lawyers accept the case on a contingency basis, you will run out of money within a few months.

This strategy has been perfected and is unbeatable. You are a mildly annoying fly that got into the stable of a $100M race horse. You will be squashed. You have no chance.

Actually, you have one small chance. Almost negligibly small. If you sue ABM for patent interference, you can ask for a jury trial. If you can make it that far, the jury members will not be corporate moguls. Corporate moguls don't serve on juries because they can't be bothered. In any event, they won't serve on the jury of your case because they will be disqualified. Lawyers who make $10M salaries can't serve on juries because they're lawyers. So the men and women in the jury pool will be people who make $40K per year, maybe more or maybe less. They are pretty much like you. Maybe they've had a dream of inventing something and making a sale. ABM's lawyers will be in court wearing Armani suits, and you will be there in your Men's Warehouse corduroy sport coat. Maybe it has threadbare sleeves.

Going head to head against Mammoth Semiconductor Inc. is rarely a good idea. But you can leverage your advantage. Mammoth Semiconductor might be an 800 pound gorilla and you are a fly. But there are likely to be several 300 pound gorillas. Each of these is looking for ammunition. They won't go to court against Mammoth. But they are looking to build their IP portfolio up so they can have more leverage at the bargaining table. This is why they may be willing to talk to you.

This leads us to the most important US patent ever granted: the *submarine patent.*

CHAPTER

4

Patents On Submarines

Perhaps the most famous of the pioneering underwater vessels that have become known as submarines was the "Turtle." It was built by two graduates of Yale, David Bushnell and Phineas Pratt. It was called "Turtle" because it resembled a sea-turtle floating vertically in the water. If you've ever watched a turtle for a while, you know that it sometimes floats this way with its nose just breaking the surface. The Turtle was not built for exploration nor to prove that a boat didn't have to float on top of the water. It was built in 1776 during the War of Independence. Its purpose was to attack the British Navy. It functioned successfully as a submarine, but had approximately zero success with wartime missions.

Bushnell and Pratt really developed two inventions: The first was an underwater bomb, which was the world's first and which they called a torpedo. The second was the underwater vessel to deliver it. The technology used many innovations. There was a flintlock detonator that was very much like the mechanism on a musket. It was connected to a timer so the Turtle could attach the torpedo to the target ship and then safely retreat before it blew up. The interior of the Turtle vessel was lined with phosphorescent wood, a clever way to provide dim interior light for the operator.

The first attack was on a British ship in NY harbor in the early morning of Sept. 7, 1776. With Sgt. Ezra Lee operating the vessel, the Turtle worked just as it was supposed to and approached a ship without being seen. However, the torpedo was supposed to attach to the hull with a screw. The screw hit metal instead of wood and he failed to attach the device. The Turtle was seen and Sgt. Lee successfully made a retreat. The mission was not a complete failure. The British were confounded by the strange vessel and they moved their fleet out of New York Harbor. The Turtle made a second outing. Again it was detected by sailors on the target ship and the ship gave chase. Sgt. Lee detached the torpedo and it detonated in open water. The British stopped their pursuit and the Turtle escaped again.

Interest in developing a submarine grew in the 19th century. Lodner D. Phillips built at least two submarines in the 1850s. Each was powered by a hand-cranked screw (propeller). The first collapsed at a depth of 20 feet. The second reached a depth of about 100 feet and achieved an underwater speed of 4 knots. Phillips offered to sell his invention to the US Navy. The Navy responded: "No authority is known to this Bureau to purchase a submarine boat … the boats used by the Navy go on, not under, the water." Phillips was granted a patent in 1852 for a "Steering Submarine Propellar."[1] The particular innovation central to the patent was a means for steering the submarine, both left and right as well as up-and-down. This was achieved by using a hand-cranked propeller that was mounted on a swivel joint.

The U.S. Navy gradually changed its mind about submarines. The Navy announced submarine design competitions in 1887 and 1888 with the goal of developing a viable submarine. Inventor John P. Holland won both competitions. On both occasions, Holland faced contractual and funding problems that blocked his hopes of building a prototype. Holland also won a third competition, held in 1893. Following this, in the mid and late 1890s, Holland designed and built several prototype submarines. One had three steam engines for propulsion. Unfortunately there was so much heat from the engines that it was impossible for anyone to be inside. Holland next designed a dual propulsion system.

There was an internal combustion engine for use on the surface, and electric motors powered by batteries for use when submerged. This basic model is still used today. The only superior technology is nuclear powered submarines and they weren't introduced until the 1950s. Holland's prototype, named "Holland," reached a speed of 7 knots on the surface (pretty good), and could remain submerged for several hours. It was designed to remain slightly buoyant when the ballast tanks were full. The U.S. Navy bought the Holland and commissioned it in 1900 as the *USS Holland*. It was used for testing and design research for 13 years. His patent, US patent 708,553, is dated 1902 even though he had successful trial runs as early as 1899.[2]

Simon Lake was another entrant in the 1893 design competition. Lake's proposal described a vessel to be used for commercial applications like salvage. It was designed to sink below the surface when the ballast tanks were full. It had wheels so that it could roll across the ocean floor. Propulsion was to be provided by a steam engine that would be shut down when the vessel was submerged. When submerged, compressed air would be used to turn both the propeller and wheels. Several prototypes were built and Lake was granted U.S. Patent No. 531,213 (1897) for a "Submarine Vessel."[3]

By the end of the 19th century a rivalry had developed between Holland and Lake. The prize would be a lucrative contract with the US Navy. Holland had formed the "Electric Boat Company." Lake started the "Lake Torpedo Boat Company." Both companies built prototypes that began to resemble the submarines of the 20th century. They were relatively large and complex. Lake's submarine *Protector* was 65 feet long and displaced 170 tons. It had two screws, two gasoline engines that powered the boat on the surface, and batteries for two electric motors to power it while submerged. It even had a crude periscope. Holland sold his submarine *Holland VI* to the Navy in 1890. Lake made his first sale to Russia. The competition between Holland and Lake continued for decades. Though both companies sold submarines to the US Navy, Holland is generally considered the father of the modern submarine.

There have been many crucial patents that led to the submarines that have been so successful for oceanographic research and warfare in the twentieth century. Of course, none of these is related in any way to the world's most important patent, the *submarine patent*. This chapter is a red herring, though I hope it has been informative. A *submarine patent* is a type of patent and it's become associated with a particular business strategy. The first submarine patents involved barcodes.

CHAPTER

5

The Submarine Patent

The first *submarine patent* was one in a portfolio of patents that changed patent law. It also led to one of the largest cases of intellectual property litigation of the twentieth century.

Who is the greatest American inventor of all time? The first name that would come to mind is Thomas Edison. Edison had 1,093 patents in his name at the time of his death. He seems to be the quintessential inventor, giving society inventions such as the phonograph and the light bulb. But that's the problem with Edison: He is the quintessential inventor and that's bad. Edison started out as an independent garage inventor. As his successes grew, he changed his business model. He set up a laboratory and hired people to work there. Many of his workers provided extra hands for his ideas. Edison referred to them as "muckers." As time went on, he hired more brilliant and inventive workers. They had ideas. But Edison's business model held that anyone who worked for him, using his tools and receiving his wages, gave up their IP to the company. And Edison was the company. Some very smart inventors worked for Edison. Examples are Nicolai Tesla (Edison Machine Works) and Henry Ford (Edison Illuminating Company, Detroit).

Thomas Edison invented a way of inventing. There were others who worked this way, but Edison was very successful with it. It was a hierarchical scheme, with Edison at the top. It involved a group, rather than an individual, and it was multi-disciplinary. Some of his team received rewards in the form of stock in the company and this allowed talented team members to succeed financially in proportion with the company. This model was later copied by Intel and, more recently, by numerous software startup companies. The downside is that it's an autocratic model. Robert Noyce, one of the founders of Intel and a Nobel laureate, made the observation "There is a basic incompatibility between the inventor and the large corporation[1]...." The worker's rights go to the company, and the agenda is set by the company and the owner (Edison, in this case). The brightest and most independent workers, who have their own ideas, leave the company. Examples are Tesla and Ford. In the bigger picture, the worst aspect of this model, that all individual rights are given to the company, has been adopted by almost all companies. The best aspect, the chance for individual talent to rise and to receive just compensation, has not been adopted by most companies.

America's greatest inventor was a man who invented a different way of inventing. His goal was to establish a way for the independent inventor to work for himself, a way for the little guy to have protection for his intellectual property. His greatest invention was the *submarine patent*. This brings us to the first submarine patent. Actually, there was a portfolio of submarine patents. The first submarine patent portfolio started with patents concerning automated warehouses, conveying systems and inventory control. It ended with barcodes. Before we get to the submarine portfolio, let's start with some stories about the invention of barcodes and barcode readers. That was the focus of the court case.

As we begin this story, remember that large corporations seek first and foremost to destroy every spark of independent invention. Corporate leaders and their attorneys dismember puppies and immolate kittens. And they enjoy it.

There are many patents that led to the development of barcodes and barcode readers. A seminal patent was the result of two co-inventors, Norman Joseph Woodland and Bernard Silver. Woodland was a mechanical engineer who had worked on the Manhattan project. He and Silver were graduate students in a master's program at Drexel University in Philadelphia. In 1948, a local supermarket executive visited Drexel, met with the Dean and asked him to develop an automated technique for encoding product data. The Dean passed the problem on to some of the students. Woodland and Silver came up with the idea of putting a unique code on every item of merchandise, a code that could be easily scanned by a mechanical device. Their patent, titled "Classifying Apparatus and Method," was issued about 3 years after the filing date of Oct. 20, 1949.[2] They got a lot of things right. They invented a code of light and dark bars of different widths and arranged with a pattern of locations, and they described how to use these patterns to represent binary digital information. This part was Woodland's idea. He told the story that he was sitting in the sand on a beach near Miami thinking about the problem. He had learned Morse code in his childhood. He stuck the four digit fingers of one hand in the sand, then pulled his hand in towards his body. The four lines in the sand gave him a vision for how to make a bar code – multiple lines of different widths, where the width (narrow or wide) represented a binary 0 or 1 (dot or dash).[3] Woodland and Silver knew about using photo-cells as readers. They described an application in which the barcode and reader could be used to read prices. The barcode also could be linked to broader functions. They described conveyor belts that would carry the coded items over the reader and then sort the items by code. Items with a given code could be deflected to other conveyor belts and moved to a specified location. Barcodes would be used for many different things, for example parts on an assembly line, and not just merchandise.

The Woodland and Silver invention was ahead of its time. However, it was not really workable for the technology that was available in the 1950s and 60s. One large problem was that it required a very bright (500 watt) light source. They sold the patent to Philco for $15,000. The patent was never enforced. It expired in 1969 before there was viable technology to commercialize it. Woodland got a job at IBM in 1951, and worked there for the next 36 years.

The big break for barcode technology came with the development of the laser.[3] Lasers will be discussed in Chapter 7. For now, the historical importance is that the first laser was demonstrated by Theodore Maiman of Hughes Aircraft in July, 1960. His apparatus was big and ugly. "It looks like something a plumber made," remarked the head of public relations for Hughes.[3] But there had been intense international competition to build the first laser and this first successful demonstration fueled the interest of scientists around the world. Every lab with an optics division had a laser group. Reliable lasers were commercially available by 1970. These were smaller than a bread-box and had a reasonable price tag of roughly a few hundred dollars. One perfect application for the laser was the barcode reader. The beam was bright and almost perfectly collimated. In other words, the light did not spread out. Instead, all the intensity was in a narrow beam that could be aimed at a barcode. The laser was quickly adapted and barcode readers were first used in supermarkets in 1974. The first reader in commercial use was the NCR 255 Scanning System made by National Cash Register. It included a scanner and mini computer. Each mini computer was linked to an NCR 726 computer at a central location in the store. The system could be used at cash register check-out and also for inventory control.

One of NCR's biggest competitors was RCA. A group at RCA was looking for projects. Kroger, a grocery store chain, had announced their interest in any mechanized procedure that would speed the check-out process. The RCA group was looking through the patent data base. This is commonly called trolling. It's a technique that large companies have used for years. They have a person (or a small group of people) who searches through patents looking for those that show good ideas and have no assignments. If a patent has expired or if a patent is not assigned to a corporation, then the company can take the idea and run with it. In the former case, the ideas are in the public domain. In the latter case, they don't worry about the rights of an independent inventor who cannot mount resistance against infringement. In either case, they can develop the idea and create their own IP portfolio. The RCA group came across the Woodland patent. RCA had a laser group and they started working on a prototype. A successful test was run in a Kroger store in Cincinnati in 1972.[3]

Now there were two competing products commercially available, with other prototypes in development. Representatives of the grocery trade got together and formed a committee that was supposed to find a way to introduce and standardize a Universal Product Code (UPC), a bar code of some kind that would be imprinted by the manufacturers and retailers and would be common to all goods sold in supermarkets. The code for any item would carry basic information including a product identifier and the company that made it. Scanners in a store would "read" this information and link it to an in-store computer. The computer would have price information along with inventory data. They could program the computer to make special offers that depended on inventory. The grocery trade had a vision but didn't know how it would be realized. They went to the high tech community for help.

Seven companies submitted barcode proposals to the committee. RCA was confident it would win the endorsement but IBM surprised them all and entered the competition. IBM had no prior interest in barcodes, scanners or the grocery business in general. However, Jerome Woodland was now working at IBM. His colleague, George J. Laurer, came up with a proposal for a code that fit inside a rectangle, based on the Woodland-Silver model. The Committee decided in favor of IBM and gave them a list of specifications for size, number of coded digits, and an allowed error rate during reading. Laurer designed a barcode within the specifications. A division of IBM then built a prototype scanner. Laurer printed a number of barcode labels and attached them to beanbag ash trays, on the bottom of the beanbag. As a test of the system, an IBM colleague would toss the ash trays over the scanner as fast as he could. The scanner read the code without fail, regardless of the speed of the toss or the orientation of the rectangular label. The trick is that a small subset of the bars in the bar code is used by the computer to determine the speed and orientation of the label. The computer then uses that information to interpret the other bars. The Laurer barcode was adopted as an industry standard in 1973.

The Universal Product Code was not an immediate success. Small grocery stores could not afford the scanner and didn't really need it because their inventories were small. Kmart was the first large chain store to implement the UPC. Others followed after that. Scanners finally took off in the 1980s. By 2004, about 85% of the top 500 retail companies in the US were using the UPC. The larger impact came from the spread of the technology. For retail stores, the data could be used to understand trends of what was selling, where, and for how much. But the technology spread beyond retailers. Barcodes and scanners were used for inventory control anywhere there was an inventory. This included warehouses and factories.

That leads us to the other story of barcodes and barcode scanners. It's also the story of the submarine patent.

Jerome Lemelson grew up in Staten Island, New York. His childhood goal was to be an inventor like Thomas Edison. He started university at New York University, then was called to serve in the Army Air Corps in World War 2. He completed a Bachelor's degree in Aeronautical Engineering after the war, and then Masters degrees in Aeronautical Engineering and Industrial Engineering, also at NYU. He graduated and took a job at Republic Aviation designing guided missiles. He also began dabbling with inventions.

In 1951 he saw a demonstration of an automatic metal lathe that was controlled by instructions from punch cards. This led to an interest in the concept of automated industrial machines. He formed a vision for a universal machine that could perform multiple functions, such as measurement, assembly (welding, for example), and finally quality control inspection. Taking the broad view, he saw his ideas as an entirely new technology that he called "machine vision." Machine vision would combine information input in the form of digitized information sensed by photocells with computers that would analyze the input data and control subsequent process steps. The photo cells would later be replaced by video cameras. It would take him several years to develop this complex idea. In the meantime, he filed some simpler patent applications that offered a chance to get some income from licensing royalties.

Lemelson's first patents, and the first patents to be licensed, issued in the early 1950s and were for children's toys. The IP climate in the 1950s was not sympathetic to independent garage inventors. One of his first experiences with patents and licensing involved a case of infringement where Lemelson was on the losing end. It started with an idea he had for a face mask for a child that could be printed on the back of a cardboard cereal box and then cut out. He filed a patent application and took his idea to a large cereal manufacturer. The company rejected Lemelson's pitch. About three years later, the same company began using cereal boxes with cut-out face masks printed on the back. Lemelson was shocked when he first saw one of these boxes on a grocery store shelf. He believed this was a clear case of patent infringement. He filed a patent interference suit, which promptly was dismissed in court. He appealed, and it was dismissed again.[4] This defeat, and his frustration with the injustice behind the loss, had a big effect on Lemelson. He resolved to find a way to defend his IP rights and, in the process, to defend the rights of independent inventors against the power of large corporations. He succeeded. Over a span of about 45 years he sought court action in about 20 cases. Although he lost more often than he won, his cases set precedents.

Lemelson didn't have enough money to hire a patent attorney so he wrote his own patent applications. He taught himself how to write the specification and claims and learned the ins and outs of the entire legal process. He drafted the figures himself. He was a one-man operation. He worked on his "machine vision" idea for three years before completing two related applications in 1954. He filed an application titled "Automatic Warehousing System" on July 28, 1954, serial no. 449,874. This worked its way through the system and was issued Jan. 28, 1964, as US Patent No. 3,119,501. It describes an automated warehouse in which carriers (called carriages in the patent, they look like forklifts in the figures) are suspended and move on tracks mounted in the ceiling. The movements of the carriages are controlled and tracked by sensors and electric circuits. Of specific interest, the patent includes a description of photoelectric scanners and reflective markers. Five months later he filed a 150 page long application, on Dec. 24, 1954, that was titled "Automatic Devices," serial no. 477,467. This application was later abandoned, but some of the ideas were included in new filings.

A typical patent application might have a specification with a length between 4 and 15 pages. In the 1950s, it might take the USPTO one to three years to complete the examination process. Most of that time the application was simply waiting to reach an Examiner's desk. The Examiner can do more than simply accept or reject claims. An application that covers a complex idea and is described with a long specification is often broken up into several applications, each describing an aspect of the overall invention. Each of these applications derived from the original is called a divisional application. Furthermore, the inventor can file a new application as a "continuation" or "continuation in part" of an existing application. For a continuation, the specification of the existing application cannot be changed but the inventor can change or add claims, as long as the claims are supported by the existing specification. For a "continuation in part," the inventor keeps the original specification (either explicitly or by reference) and then may add new material in the form of text and/or figures, as well as new claims. In the era of 1950s through the 1980s, a complicated patent application that had divisionals and continuations might take 10 to 20 years for the PTO to complete the examination and issue a patent. In this era, the PTO did not publish applications. They only published a patent after it had been granted and issued. A competitor interested in the technology related to such a patent would have no knowledge of the details of the patent for 10 to 20 years, until the patent (or patents) was issued. This kind of patent became known as a *submarine patent* precisely because it was invisible to the competitors. Its stealth became a key strategic attribute in the intellectual property battles.

"Automatic Devices" was broken into divisional applications, along with continuations. Serial no. 477,467 was abandoned, but a number of related applications worked their way through the PTO. Lemelson filed several other lengthy applications during the early 1950s. For example, an application for an "Automatic Measurement Apparatus," serial no. 626,211 was filed Dec. 4, 1956. This application was issued as a patent with the same name, patent no. 3,081,379, on March 12, 1963. It describes using video cameras to detect and measure characteristics of a product in an assembly line. The cameras are linked to a computer. The detection might involve a range of functions from determining the location of an object to quality control measurements. An example of the division and continuation process is patent no. 4,118,730 titled "Scanning apparatus and method." This patent is a continuation in part that cites both applications 477,467 and 626,211 and also cites patent 3,081,379. It was filed May 18, 1972 and issued on Oct. 3, 1978. This patent and later continuations of this patent are at the heart of the barcode battle. The new material in 4,118,730 includes a figure that shows a conveyor belt with a scanner (video camera) mounted overhead. The added text describes a method by which the scanned image is recorded as a binary string of information (equivalently, a binary code). The scanner is connected to a central computer. The binary codes for a variety of objects are stored in computer memory. The object can be identified by comparing the code that is read by the scanner with the codes stored in memory.

In this patent, Lemelson describes the technique of scanning an object for the purpose of identification. In the context of an automated assembly line or warehouse, this information is used for controlling the movement of the object from one place to another, which thereby controls the processes that are applied to the object. It also may control storage and inventory. Figure 16 in 4,118,730 begins to resemble early figures describing supermarket barcode scanners, and this becomes the heart of the controversy. RCA ran the first test of a supermarket scanner in 1972, the same year that Lemelson filed 4,118,730. The question can be raised: how much did Lemelson know about the parallel developments of scanner technology that were aimed at supermarket checkout stands?

Lemelson had licensing agreements with large companies, for example Sony and Texas Instruments, concerning his IP in the area of magnetic recording. These agreements gave him a good income but he was not rich. Not yet. In 1983 the automobile manufacturers in the US met and adopted a uniform standard for the barcodes that were used in their warehouses and assembly lines. Lemelson hired an attorney to help him with litigation. This attorney sent letters to the major companies in the automobile industry (and others) notifying them that they were infringing on his barcode and warehouse / assembly line management patents. In 1992, Lemelson settled with the major Japanese automobile companies. His attorney settled with about 40 other industrial companies. He netted about $0.5B from these deals. Now he was wealthy. More broadly, the litigation and settlements were of tremendous importance. They forged entirely new paths in the business of patent law.

Jerome Lemelson died in 1997. In 1998, the big three US auto companies settled with the Lemelson Estate (Lemelson Medical, Education, and Research Foundation). And then the tides changed. In a classic case of over-reach, the Lemelson Foundation sued 400 companies, including the large retail companies Target and Walmart, for patent infringement for the barcode scanners they used in their checkout lines. Two companies that made and sold checkout belt scanning systems, Cognex and Symbol, filed counter suits. In 2004, a federal district court in Nevada ruled against the Lemelson Estate. It ruled that Lemelson's "machine vision" patents were invalid and unenforceable. In the big picture, the Cognex v. Lemelson Foundation ruling was just as important as the settlement Lemelson received 12 years earlier. The submarine strategy was established, but the Cognex ruling imposed limits.

Here we have the two sides of the submarine patent debate. Lemelson's attorneys argued that he had the vision of the concept of a barcode and scanning system, and he described the system in enough detail that others in the field could understand the unique merits of such a system. Cognex and Symbol argued that Lemelson gamed the patent process. He cheated by writing continuation patents that adapted aspects of his original idea. But his continuations used developments that had been made by others and to which he had no claim. In the end, the court's decision turned on the testimony of expert witnesses who agreed that the body of Lemelson's patents did not include enough specific information that would permit an expert to build the commercial barcode scanner in use in 2004.

Of course, the same experts would have to view the Woodland and Silver patent in the same way. It did not include enough specific information that would permit an expert to build the commercial barcode scanner in use in 2004.

Woodland and Silver are generally recognized as the main inventors of bar code technology. Woodland received the National Medal of Technology and Innovation in 1992. He was inducted into the National Inventors Hall of Fame in 2011. Silver was inducted, posthumously, at the same time.[5] There are two key reasons why Woodland and Silver were given recognition as the main inventors of this technology. The first is that they had the basic idea for barcodes and readers and articulated the concept clearly in their patent. The second is that their patent was never enforced. Had the patent been enforced, they would have made a lot of enemies – basically everyone associated with an enterprise that was forced to pay royalties (note that "pay" does not necessarily mean a cash transaction). Lemelson, and later his heirs, pushed to enforce his patents and he made a lot of enemies. He probably pushed too far. The machine vision patents for warehouse and assembly line scanners may have held up in court.

The major corporations crush independent inventors and take their ideas all the time. This creates a lot of enemies. But these enemies are independent inventors who have been crushed and have no money, so you never hear from them.

The PTO changed the law regarding patent applications. In 2000, they enacted a rule that patent applications would be published in public PTO files. With such publication, submarine patents are no longer invisible. Some basic "submarine" strategies still exist, and these techniques promote the rights of individual and independent inventors. The following paragraphs provide an example of the subtle issues surrounding the use of submarine patents. This example concerns touchscreen technology and it is entirely fiction. The story is fiction. It is not accurate about any of the details surrounding the way touchscreens work, the associated technological advances and the people who made them.

Joe is a graduate student doing materials science research. He's working with indium tin oxide (ITO), a transparent oxide material that is capable of conducting electricity. He discovers a process for lithographic patterning and fabrication of thin film ITO wires. This gives him the idea for an invention: a touch screen. His idea is the following. He starts with a thin, clear sheet of plastic that's fairly strong but not too stiff. He fabricates an array of parallel ITO wires along one axis (call it the x-axis) on one side of the plastic. He fabricates the same array of ITO wires oriented along a perpendicular axis (call it the y-axis) on the other side. The typical width and pitch (spacing from edge of one wire to edge of the neighbor wire) of the wires is 1 mm. He puts this on a substrate and deposits a thin, transparent, protective film on top. His idea is that every pair of top and bottom wires forms a capacitor at the intersection of the two wires, i.e. at location (x, y). The capacitance is A/s where A is the area of the intersection (one square mm) and s is the distance between the two wires (the thickness of the plastic sheet). He can touch the top surface and the thin film wires that are near his finger depress the clear plastic in the middle. Remember, the clear plastic is "not too stiff." It's soft enough to deform a little under the pressure of a touch. The distance s changes, and the capacitance of all the capacitors formed by intersections near his finger will show a change of capacitance. A circuit on a chip can monitor the capacitance of the array constantly. For example, a small voltage can be applied across a resistor to every wire on top, and every wire on the bottom can have a similar resistance between the wire and ground. The voltage measured across each intersection will be proportional to the capacitance there. The chip then records that the capacitors near (x,y) had a change of value and the chip can interpret the results to mean that an input was made at (x,y).

Joe writes a patent disclosure. His university, which owns the rights to his research, says it will never work and they won't file an application. Now he's free to file an application on his own.

He does. He writes an application. The broad idea is to have two arrays of transparent conducting wires on opposite sides of a transparent insulator such that the intersection of each pair of wires forms a capacitor. Changes in the capacitance of any capacitor can be sensed and interpreted as an input at a specific location. He presents the preferred embodiment using the above description. He notes that there might be other materials and other geometries that would achieve the same results. In the claims, the broadest claim is for an array of transparent conducting wires on top of a thin transparent insulator, an array on the bottom, circuits for monitoring the capacitance between top wire x and bottom wire y, and a small logic circuit that interprets the change of capacitance as an input signal at (x,y). The claims are accepted and patent 1000 is granted.

Company ABM invites Joe to give a talk about the fabrication of ITO wires and circuits. He mentions the idea of arrays of wires during his visit. ABM instructs their patent trolls to investigate the status of IP.

They find his patent and report that it's an open field because his patent is not assigned to a company.

ABM starts a research effort on touch screen technology. They confirm that arrays of wires form capacitors at the intersecting points, but they make a new discovery. It's not necessary to change the distance s between the two conductors. A finger always carries a small amount of static charge. When the finger touches the top wire of the array, a small amount of charge is transferred to the wire and that small charge changes the capacitance of the capacitor formed by the intersecting wires. They write a dozen patents on different aspects of their version of the invention and go into production.

By accident, Joe reads a report in a technology newsletter that describes a new product, a touchscreen, that is soon to be introduced to the market. The report mentions that ITO is used for the wires and it mentions that the transparent plastic used between the arrays has been a topic of research at ABM. The article does not give any details about this plastic, but Joe infers that this layer is probably important to ABM's version of the touch screen. Joe writes a "continuation" patent that uses the specification in his original patent and then adds some more specific claims. The list includes claims for specific materials, such as ITO for the arrays. He then lists a variety of commercial plastics, both soft and rigid, as the material that can be used between arrays. The claims are accepted and patent 1001 is granted. One of the materials he listed happens to be the material that ABM is using.

A couple of years later, Joe hires an attorney who contacts ABM and tells them they are infringing on Joe's IP. They ignore him. Joe's attorney points out that the broad claim in patent 1000 covers the embodiment that they have commercialized, and further notes that they are infringing on specific claims in patent 1001. ABM replies that Joe doesn't deserve anything because the preferred embodiment that was described in patent 1000 describes a *rigid* transparent plastic between the two arrays, and does not describe the mechanism of changing the capacitance by *transferring charge from a finger*. Joe's attorney responds that the specification is not legally enforceable. Rather, the claims are legally enforced. Joe's claims in patent 1000 are a valid and accurate description of the ABM device, and his specific claims in patent 1001, which include the materials that ABM is using, are supported by the broadly general descriptions in the specification of patent 1000. A person "skilled in the art" could make the touchscreen that ABM sells by using the information in Joe's two patents.

Who is right? It doesn't matter. What matters is who will win. The viewpoint of ABM is that broad ideas belong to everyone and what really matters is who puts in the work that's needed to bring an idea to market as a successful product. Joe's opinion is that all ideas that are succinctly described are protected by patent law. ABM had no ideas about touch screens until he mentioned something during his visit and, later, when they read his patent. Joe deserves something for having the original idea. ABM deserves something for doing the work to refine the idea. But ABM was awarded a dozen patents on many aspects of their version of the touch screen, and those patents ensure that ABM will make money from their development work. Joe's attorney tells him that he would have little chance of winning a suite for infringement based on the single broad claim in patent 1000. However, patents 1000 and 1001 together have 6 or 7 claims that interfere with ABM's IP and it will be hard for ABM to beat all of them. In the end, Western Big Company (WBC) has plans to start making touch screens and they purchase Joe's patents. They will use them to barter with ABM and diminish the IP costs of their product. They can buy Joe's patents for $5M and he's happy. It may end up saving them the equivalent of $100M in license fees, or maybe not. WBC doesn't seem to care. The expense is lost in their accounting and never shows up as lost income.

CHAPTER

6

Inventors in Industrial Labs

The independent inventor has no standing in the world of corporate intellectual property behemoths, but what's it like for a scientist inventor who works for an industrial lab? I was one of those and was (briefly) very happy.

My life changed the day I accepted the Swell Labs offer. They treated me first class in every way. Once I was hired, they paid for a trip to New Jersey to look at housing. Then they arranged for a moving company to move all my possessions. Actually I had few possessions, but they drove my car into a moving van and moved it, plus a desk, a few milk crates and several boxes of books, to New Jersey. Swell arranged for a small suite at a Residence Hotel near the lab for my first two weeks. They sent me an airline ticket. They paid for a limo to take me to the airport. They arranged for a limo service to meet me at Newark airport, and the limo drove me to my Residence hotel. I took up residence in the middle of August. Swell arranged for a rental car for me to use while my car was in transit from the west coast.

My first day as a Member of Technical Staff (MTS) at Swell began with a new employee orientation meeting at corporate headquarters.

I had been given a packet of information with a bunch of forms to fill out. I filed into the meeting room with about twenty other new employees at 8:00 in the morning. Swell Labs was not a single facility at a single site. Swell operated five labs at five different locations. This orientation was for new science staff employees, representing all the different facilities. The HR woman who directed the meeting was very efficient. She'd done this many times before. We went through all the forms. Retirement program. Health insurance. Life insurance. We reviewed the ethics standards. And then there was intellectual property (IP). We went through the IP forms. We were asked if we had any disclosures or patent applications that had been filed and were in progress. I raised my hand and described a disclosure I'd written as a postdoc, noting that the university where I worked had declined to file an application. I was told to check "no" on the form. Someone else raised his hand and mentioned a disclosure. The HR woman talked with him for a few minutes. She then adjourned the meeting for ten minutes, telling us to stretch our legs and get coffee. Meanwhile, this new hire was led to a phone where he called one of Swell's IP lawyers. It was clear that Swell took IP very seriously.

The meeting continued. The HR woman explained the policy that was described on our forms. We would relinquish all rights to our IP and assign these rights to Swell in return for a monetary payment. The payment was one dollar. After explaining the policy, she walked around the room and gave each of us a one dollar bill. Each of us signed a receipt for the one dollar we received. I still have that dollar – I've kept it in my desk drawer with a sticky note attached. Then we signed the form that assigned our IP to Swell, having received "fair and just" compensation.

There was no employment contract among all the forms. Instead, there were agreements. There was no protection against termination by Swell. Swell labs had the right to terminate you for any reason at almost any time. There were yearly merit reviews. You could be terminated if you did not fare well on these reviews. Furthermore, Swell had the right to move their work force. They could decide that one facility should be downsized and another should be upsized. They could terminate your employment if needed for these kinds of changes. For any termination, they had to give you 60 days minimum notice.

One of the new employees raised his hand and asked the question that crossed the minds of most of us. Was it really fair that Swell should get all the rights to our IP? The HR woman obviously had heard this question before. She was quick to describe the deal that Swell presented to us. The Swell scientist would be well paid and would be able to do any basic research that he/she wanted to do, and would do it at the most prestigious lab in the world. All we had to do was publish our results in distinguished journals, and we had to publish at an acceptable rate. In return, Swell got our IP rights. She explained that ninety-nine percent of basic research had no technological consequences. Swell needed to get all our rights so that it could exploit the one percent of results that had marketable implications. She said that we'd have great careers as long as we published at an acceptable rate.

The deal sounded good to me and everyone else in the room. I signed up with no further thought. She was lying.

Fine print is important. It turns out that these forms also had a lot of fine print. Things that the HR person didn't have time to talk about. Later on (a couple of years later), I read the fine print. There was something very important there: if I were to separate voluntarily from Swell, for example if I resigned in order to take a different job, I would be forbidden to do research that was related to my work at Swell Labs for a period of two years. If separation from Swell was not voluntary, meaning that Swell instigated the separation, then there would be no restrictions on my research after termination. That single paragraph in 6 point font would turn out to be important. It allowed me to become an independent inventor and led directly to my windfall.

About a year later on a fine spring day the Associate Vice President (AVP) of the lab called a lab-wide meeting for that afternoon. This seemed unusual to me. Large meetings were usually called after a day or two of advance notice. There was palpable tension in the room. The AVP announced that the directors of the lab had decided to downsize our facility. He told us what would happen. Head count would be reduced. Positions would be eliminated. Those who held those positions would be declared to be "surplus." The positions they had held had been removed and therefore they were not needed. Some institutions used the term *reduction in force* (RIF). Many places use the common term layoff. The term at Swell was "surplus." It was not the same as a layoff because there was no expectation, indeed no possibility, of reclaiming your position later. It was basically the same as a RIF. The *surplus* MTSs would have time to choose between three options. Option 1: Swell would come up with a different position that they could accept, but that position might require a change of research field. Option 2: Swell would offer them a severance package. They could accept the package (a monetary sum that was scaled with the years of service) and then voluntarily leave by a negotiated date. Option 3: the MTS would be declared to be surplus. The MTS would be terminated with no severance compensation.

The RIFs were announced in waves. One round was announced in November. Management held a meeting for all MTSs, with the stated goal of helping us adjust to the new situation. One of the managers was giving a talk. He said "The days when you could study your thesis topic for your entire professional life are over. You have to be flexible. You have to be able to branch out to different areas of research." I was listening to this. I had been trained in optics and compound semiconductors and I thought he meant I might have to branch out into applied optics or silicon device physics. I figured I could adjust to that, grudgingly. But then someone asked what areas were relevant to the new direction that Swell Labs was taking. He said "Software." Whoa! Stop right there! Software is not a branch of research physics. It's an entirely different discipline. Changing to software represented a career change. What if I learned enough software to be relevant to Swell and then Swell folded and I lost my job? I would be out on the street competing for software jobs with those who had a Ph. D. or a Masters degree in software. I would have no chance. And I would have given up physics, with no road back to a research profession.

I had been the last person to join the lab and I was one of the last dozen to leave. The end was rather chaotic. Ninety percent of the staff scientists had gone and that included 90 percent of managers. My management chain was changing every month. No one ever approached me to help me make plans. I did not step forward and volunteer to resign. One day in early December I received a fat envelope in my inbox. When I opened it there was a pink slip on top. Yes, pink slips really are pink. I was given 60 days notice of my termination. It was not a very happy Christmas. A week after I separated from Swell I phoned a patent attorney and became an independent inventor.

CHAPTER

7

The Telecommunications Platform

We've seen that many people in high technology made a lot of money and others didn't. Let's see what some of the key people did and how they failed or succeeded in making a fortune. Information technology is a broad term, comprising digital information processing and communications. It is built on a physical platform that has many parts. There are computers of all kinds, from personal desktops and laptops to main frames, and mobile devices including digital audio players, cell phones and tablets for information processing. There are phone lines, cables, optic fibers and radio waves for communicating digital information. There are many inventions that enabled the information technology revolution. I will review some history and then discuss several inventions that were keystones in the creation of this platform. Two of these are closely related and, together, created an entirely new mode of communication.

Fiber optic network - optic fiber wires and diode lasers

Humans transmitted information orally or by print for millennia. It was a revolution when mankind learned to transmit information electronically. This didn't happen until the nineteenth century, first by telegraph (Samuel Morse, 1830s), then by telephone (Alexander Graham Bell, 1870s) and by radio waves (Heinrich Hertz and Guglielmo Marconi, 1890s). For a century electronic transmission used lines made with an electrical conductor (like copper) or waves propagated through air. The idea of propagating waves through an electrically insulating material was against the instincts and intuition of most scientists. But the technology of sending information by transmitting light waves through glass, in the form of optic fibers, was a revolution with an impact whose magnitude is so large (and still growing) that it can't yet be measured.

Like most paradigm shifting technologies, there were many contributions to the development of optical transmission. But what motivated the pioneers even to pursue the possibility? The answer is *bandwidth*, which describes the amount of information that can be transmitted per second through a *transmission line* such as a phone line or TV cable.[1] There are some apples and oranges issues about the rigorous definition of bandwidth or of a broader term like information capacity. For now I use the term bandwidth loosely. Every electromagnetic wave has a unique frequency. You can think of bandwidth (BW), measured in hertz (Hz, named after Heinrich Rudolf Hertz and unrelated to rental cars), as the number of different frequencies (number of uniquely different waves) that a transmission line can carry. Digital information takes the form of a series of pulses. In this case, bandwidth represents the amount of binary information that can be transmitted per second. It's approximately correct to think of bandwidth as the maximum number of bits per second (bits/sec) that can be transmitted.[2] Any transmission line has a characteristic bandwidth. It's typical that a transmission system (transmitter, receiver, transmission line) is optimized for a particular frequency or range of frequencies for information transmission. I will describe this in some detail later. For now, note that for telephone transmission of a conversation, the requirement is to carry all the frequencies needed for voices. Humans can hear frequencies in the range from 10 Hz to 20 KHz, so the bandwidth needed for talking is no more than 20 KHz. In fact, one can hear voices very well using only frequencies up to about 6 KHz.

In the late 20th century, landline telephone transmission used a twisted pair transmission line (commonly called a phone line) that had a bandwidth of about 1 million Hz (1 MHz). Newer phone lines have a bandwidth of about 10 MHz. Transmission using coaxial cables had a bandwidth of about 1 GHz. Most people associate coaxial cable with the cable that goes to your television but it also carries phone transmissions. The bandwidth of single mode optic fiber, presently in use, is about 100 trillion Hz (100 THz), or 100,000 GHz.[3] To be clear, let's make the comparison. The bandwidth of optic fiber is about 100,000,000 times larger than that of twisted pair phone lines, and at least 100,000 times larger than a coaxial cable. Furthermore, the information can be transmitted more easily and with lower loss using fiber optic compared with metal wires or cables. To the few scientists who had vision, this tremendous increase in bandwidth was a big motivation.

The phone company was a highly successful business for about 100 years. It began in 1885 and was created by a very smart scientist who also was a smart businessman. It was a monopoly and that was a tremendous part of its success. The monopoly ended around 1982. How did the phone system work? The invention of the telephone has a history that includes contributions from many different individuals. It can be said that Alexander Bell was one of the dominant figures in research, and was certainly the dominant figure in commercializing the invention.

Perhaps you have heard the story about Alexander Graham Bell's famous patent. Two inventors filed a patent application for the telephone on the very same day and Bell's application was filed first by about an hour. And we all know the result. Bell became wealthy and famous and the several companies he founded were highly successful. And the guy who was an hour late? He didn't get anything. Seems to justify the old saying "A day late and a dollar short." Who was the other inventor, and is this story really true?

His name is Elisha Gray. He was a professor at Oberlin College and the simple story isn't really true. The history is more subtle. The invention of the telephone involves several distinct parts and several inventions. Most historians of science would say that a telephone must have three basic parts. (1) The sender speaks into an input mechanism that vibrates in a way that mimics the sender's vocal chords. This mechanism is a microphone. All microphones involve a diaphragm that vibrates in response to sound waves. (2) A transducer converts the vibrations into waves of electricity, also called a modulated electric current.[4] These waves form the output that is applied to (3) a means, such as a wire, that transmits the electric waves to the receiving mechanism of a second telephone. The receiver in telephone 2 performs the converse process. The electricity waves cause the diaphragm to vibrate and this creates modulated air pressure waves that are sent to the ear of the person listening to the receiver. The hardest part of inventing the telephone was making a successful microphone and transducer. Indeed, much of the history of the telephone is the same as the history of the microphone.

Gray already held a patent for an invention with a microphone / transducer that could transmit a single tone over a wire. That invention used small metal reeds placed near the poles of an electromagnet. At the sending end, the vibrating reeds would cause a modulation of the current in the electromagnet. At the receiving end, the modulated current coming into the receiver would change the magnetic field from the magnet and cause the nearby reed to vibrate. The vibration would create a tonal sound. The invention had limited use because the reeds would not respond to all frequencies. Each reed had a characteristic, *resonant* frequency. The reeds would vibrate at a few frequencies near their resonant frequencies. Tones that matched those frequencies could be transmitted, but most tones were poorly matched and were not transmitted. A human voice has a combination of many tones and could not be transmitted through Gray's invention. He sold the patent to Western Telegraph.

Gray's attorney filed a *patent caveat* (defined below) for an improved invention with a microphone / transducer that could transmit a broad range of tones and, therefore, voices. The improved invention had all three necessary parts listed above. The input used (1) a membrane that vibrated to mimic the speaker's vocal chords. For the transducer (2), the membrane was attached to a metal needle that dipped into a reservoir of water. A small amount of acid was dissolved in the water to make it electrically conducting. As the needle vibrated, its depth in the water alternated between deep and shallow and the electrical resistance, which is proportional to the depth, also modulated between weak and strong. Applying a voltage across the transducer resulted in electric waves that have the same modulation as the vibration of the membrane. The waves then could be (3) transmitted along a wire. Elisha Gray's attorney filed the patent caveat on February 14, 1876. Under patent law at that time, a *caveat* was an official notice of intention to file a patent application at a later date. It included a written description and drawings of the invention. It did not include any claims and there was no examination by the US patent office (somewhat similar to what's now called a provisional application). It was valid for a year and could be renewed by filing a $10 fee before it expired. The US patent office was located in Washington, DC. It was common to deliver applications to the patent office by hand and an inventor typically hired a patent attorney who had an office in the capital city. Gray's attorney delivered the caveat as the 39th entry of the day on February 14.

Alexander Bell's attorneys filed a full patent application on that same day. His attorney delivered the application as the fifth entry of the day. Bell's application was approved and issued three weeks later on March 7, 1876, as US patent no. 174,465, titled "Improvement in Telegraphy." Elisha Gray never renewed his caveat and never filed a patent application, even though he could have filed an application almost 11 months after Bell's patent was awarded and about ten months after Bell's first public demonstrations. As discussed below, Bell's transducer was distinctly different and it's likely that Gray could have received a patent for his liquid transducer. As of February 14, Gray had demonstrated a prototype and Bell had not. However, when Bell demonstrated his prototype in March, it worked much better Gray's transducer and telephone.

Bell's lab notes include a reference to Gray's liquid transmitter and show that he made some effort to try something similar. Bell had done only preliminary experiments on his own microphone at the time he filed his application. On March 10, he made a full laboratory test of his transmitter and receiver (transceiver). The (1) transmitter consisted of an electromagnet with a membrane nearby. A small piece of iron (armature) was glued to the middle of the membrane. As it vibrated, it (2) generated small voltages, and associated currents, in the wires of the electromagnet. This modulated current (3) was applied to a transmission line. The original transmission line was a single wire that connected to the receiver of a second telephone. The receiver also was an electromagnet, having a slightly different geometry. A diaphragm and armature was near this electromagnet. The modulated currents in this electromagnet caused the iron armature, and therefore the diaphragm, to vibrate, and this caused air pressure waves in the form of sounds that mimicked the sounds that were spoken into the transmitter.

And thus it happened, about 140 years ago, that Alexander Bell spoke into one transceiver, saying "Watson, come here. I need you." In another room, Watson heard these words on a second transceiver. Many inventors, besides Bell and Gray, had been working on devices like the early telephone. There is some speculation that Bell's attorneys were tipped off about Gray's plans and made a fortuitous filing, even though Bell had not yet successfully demonstrated his invention. There may still be some debate about how much credit Bell deserves. The answer is "a lot." After the success of Bell's invention, there were literally a thousand patent lawsuits that challenged his invention and his proprietary rights. All the challenges failed. America was a litigious culture in the 19th century, as it is today.

As a brief digression, Bell's electromagnetic microphone and transducer were soon replaced by better technology. A microphone using electrical resistance was introduced and was used for many decades. Carbon graphite is electrically conducting with a resistance much larger than a metal like copper. A small container is filled with graphite powder. A thin diaphragm is stretched over the top of the container, in contact with the powder. The diaphragm vibrates in response to sound waves. The deformations of the diaphragm apply or relieve pressure to the powder with frequencies proportional to the vibrations. The graphite powder compresses when pressure is high and the resistance of the powder in the container decreases. When the pressure is low, the powder resistance increases. Applying a voltage to the container of powder thereby results in an electric current with modulation that mimics the vibrations of the diaphragm and, therefore, the incoming sound waves. More recently, the microphone / transducer uses a variable capacitor. A capacitor (mentioned earlier in Ch. 5) is two thin metal pieces, called plates, separated by a thin layer of material that does not conduct electric current. The capacitance depends on the separation between the two plates. A microphone is made when one of the plates is a thin metal diaphragm and the material between the plates can deform by a small amount. As the diaphragm vibrates, the distance between the plates changes in proportion to the vibration. Applying a voltage to the capacitor results in an electric current with modulation that mimics the vibrations of the diaphragm. At the present time, *electret capacitor* microphones are used in both landline and cell phones. The design uses a capacitor with two plates separated by a charged dielectric (*electret*) material. They are small, inexpensive, and have good fidelity.

We've described the transmitter, composed of (1) microphone and (2) transducer, and now turn our attention to (3) the transmission line. Before we look at the details of the transmission lines of the early phone systems, a brief digression is made in order to describe some basic ideas of transmission and bandwidth.

The sounds that make up a conversation, the pixels that light up a TV screen, and other kinds of transmitted information are generically called *signals*. The signals are transmitted from one place to another as electromagnetic waves, and then converted back to their original form as a sound or picture. The process can be analog, which means using smooth waves. Or the operation can be digital, meaning the use of a stream of bits with each bit having a value of `0' or `1.' The transmission processes are similar in either case. When you speak, your voice sends out a combination of pressure waves that uses a mixture of frequencies (equivalently, wavelengths) that are mostly in the range of 10 to 10,000 Hz. Your voice represents a single channel of communication. If there are ten people in a room and all persons are talking at the same time, there are ten channels filling the room and problems of confusion arise. The same thing happens with electronic transmission. You can speak into a phone and your voice will be converted to set of electromagnetic waves with the same mix of frequencies as your voice. Your voice can be transmitted along a single wire to another phone. But sending ten such sets of electromagnetic waves along the same wire results in problems.

Similarly, you could transmit one TV signal down a coaxial cable. But sending two or three or ten TV signals down the cable would result in interference. How do you organize signals (information) so that you can efficiently transmit and receive many of them at the same time? The general term for the process is called *multiplexing* (also called *muxing*).

Let's call the set of frequencies that your voice uses a *band* of frequencies. It's the same term for the set of frequencies that a TV signal uses, and we can generalize and call it a band of information frequencies (sometimes it's called a *sideband* or *sub-band*). The solution is to add this band of frequencies to a single "strong" wave. We'll call this "strong" wave a *carrier wave*. Once we've added the information band, we say the carrier wave has been *modulated*. Then we transmit the modulated carrier wave. At the receiving end, there is a "receiver" that is "tuned" to the frequency of the carrier wave. The receiver takes the modulated wave and subtracts the pure carrier wave. Then what comes out of the receiver is just the information band, which is what we started with at the beginning. This is a fundamental concept for the process of transmission of information and involves a *transmitter*, *transmission line* and *receiver*.

An image that might help is to think of water waves. There are two kinds of water waves: gravity waves and surface tension waves. On a calm day, you can look at a lake and see small surface tension waves. They are only a few millimeters high and have a short wavelength. When the wind comes up, your attention is drawn to the larger gravity waves. They can be a foot or two high on a lake, and the wavelength can be five to fifteen feet long. The wake from a moving boat is formed by gravity waves. On a calm surface you can easily estimate the wavelength of these waves that were "transmitted" by the moving boat. If you look closely at the gravity waves, the surface waves are still there. The point of this image is to think of small waves riding on top of a larger wave. It turns out that water waves are a poor analogy because surface tension waves and gravity waves respond to different forces and therefore they don't travel together. A gravity wave can start in the middle of the lake and travel to the shore, but the surface tension waves at the middle of the lake don't travel with the wave to the shore – they just go a few feet. The surface tension waves you see near the shore are not connected to those at the middle of the lake and so, in our image, the surface tension wave is not a modulation of the gravity wave. But perhaps you can picture a band of information waves modulating a "strong" carrier wave, riding "on top" of the carrier wave, together and at the same speed. That might be a helpful image. Of course, the situation immediately becomes more complicated. With electromagnetic waves, the carrier wave is usually characterized by its frequency and not its wavelength, and the frequency of the carrier wave is modulated by the band of information frequencies. The carrier frequency is much larger than any of the frequencies in the band, by a factor of ten or a hundred or more.

The transmission of a signal using electromagnetic waves, whether analog or digital, and whether using twisted pairs or coaxial cable or microwaves broadcast into the atmosphere, uses this idea of a modulated carriers wave. Adding the sideband to the carrier is loosely called *mixing* the waves. Any given transmission line is characterized by the range of frequencies it can carry. This range is often (and confusingly) called the available *band*. That's why information bands are called *sidebands* or *sub-bands*. This range is infinite for broadcasting into space (or the atmosphere above earth). For a coaxial cable the range might be from zero to a billion Hz (1 GHz). Multiplexing is the process of dividing the available band into many different channels so that multiple signals can be sent through the same transmission line. The technique for analog waves (such as broadcast radio and television) is called *frequency-division multiplexing* (FDM). A *channel* is devoted to a single set of information, for example a single phone conversation or single TV transmission. Broadcast radio is a good example. FM radio is broadcast in the frequency range of 88 MHz to 108 MHz. This band of frequencies is divided into channels. Each channel is given a frequency range of about 200 KHz (0.2 MHz). Your favorite radio station is one such channel. Each channel has an oscillator that generates a carrier wave at the central frequency of the assigned channel. The carrier wave is "mixed" with all the waves of varying frequencies that carry the information. The result is a modulated wave (sometimes called a *baseband*) that is a mix of frequencies centered at the carrier frequency. The process of picking out a single channel and recovering the information band is called *demultiplexing* (*demuxing*). The receiver in your radio has an oscillator that can be tuned to match the carrier frequency of each baseband. It may also have a filter to eliminate a range of unwanted frequencies. Your radio tuner matches its local oscillator frequency with that of one of the carrier frequencies. The incoming baseband is *mixed* with the local oscillator with the result that the information band is removed from the carrier wave. The information band is then amplified and sent to a speaker. The carrier frequency for each channel is much larger than the sideband frequencies. For FM radio, separate channels might be found at 88.0 MHz, 88.2 MHz, 88.4 MHz, and etc. As another example, a coaxial cable might have a bandwidth of 1000 MHz (1 GHz). For analog television transmission, the sidebands for each baseband are about 5 MHz. One channel might have a carrier frequency of 900 MHz. The next channel might have a carrier frequency of 890 MHz. The next channel could have a carrier frequency of 880 MHz and so on. This idea of mixing waves to create channels is very useful. The broader concept of multiplexing in order to send many channels of information through a single transmission line is essential to telecommunications.

This same idea of multiplexing also extends to digital transmission systems. The specific process, *time domain multiplexing (TDM)*, is quite different and I won't describe it here. Almost all transmission through optic fiber is digital. As will be discussed below, the carrier wave is a coherent beam of laser light provided by a semiconductor laser. The laser can be modulated by digital electronic signals. Information processing chips can operate at speeds of several GHz. Therefore, one form of multiplexing for optic fiber transmission lines is TDM characterized by frequencies of order GHz.

But recall from the beginning of this chapter that the bandwidth of a single mode optic fiber is the order of 100 THz. How can you use all that bandwidth if you're multiplexing technology only works at frequencies of GHz, or even tens of GHz? Indeed, in the early 1980s the best multiplexing techniques were using only about 100 GHz of the available bandwidth of optic fiber. A new method, *wavelength division multiplexing (WDM)*, was working in labs by the mid 1980s. The technique is conceptually the same as FDM but is (typically) applied to lasers with wavelengths in the infrared range (roughly 1300 nm to 1500 nm). Each optic fiber transmission line carries many different infrared carrier waves. Each infrared channel carries its own set of multiplexed TDM (or FDM) signals. At the present time (2017), a commercial optic fiber transmission line might carry 400 infrared channels with each channel muxing with a band equivalent with 180 Gbit/second. That gives a net transmission rate of about 70 Tbit/sec. Improved fiber lines and WDM methods have demonstrated rates of 1,000 Tbit/sec (1 peta-bit/sec).

Returning to our history of phone service, the early commercial telephone system worked the same way that the two phones in Bell's lab worked, and the landline phone system still works the same basic way. Running transmission lines between each pair of phones becomes a bad idea as soon as you have more than two phones. Instead, you make a giant switchboard and a transmission line runs from each phone to the switchboard. Each transmission line has an identifying number (a phone number). When one phone sends a request, in the form of voltage waves, to connect with another, a person or machine connects the two transmission lines. The transmission line in the early telephone systems used a single wire strung from pole to pole. The voltage waves were sent along this wire. Voltage ground literally was the earthen ground beneath the wire. The single wire didn't work very well and by 1900 the phone company was replacing single lines with pairs of lines. One wire carried the changing voltage (the voltage wave) and the other was held at zero voltage (a reference voltage) and provided the "ground." The next innovation was the discovery that twisting the wires together improved transmission. Each wire was coated by a thin insulating layer (a fabric cladding or a layer of varnish) and then the two wires were twisted together. It might seem that twisting the wires keeps them together in a convenient way, but in fact the twisting lowers the losses, decreases noise on the line and helps prevent "cross-talk" between one pair of wires and another. In the early 1940s, the phone company began using coaxial cable for long distance transmissions. The bandwidth of early cables was about 4 MHz. This was enough for 500 phone transmissions, each baseband having a bandwidth of 8 KHz. Later, it would be enough for a single channel of television transmission.

Switchboards were automated by the middle of the 20th century. Arrays of electromechanical switches called relays were used to connect one line to another. The term switchboard went away and each large group of wires and relays was called a switch. What about long distance calls? For a relatively short distance, the call would be routed to a cable with a bundle of lines that runs to a distant location. For longer distances, the call would be routed to a microwave transmitter. AT&T began using radio transmission for some long distance calls in the late 1920s. By the early 1950s the technology for using short wavelength radio waves (microwaves) had developed. The Bell telephone system built an array of microwave transmission lines so they could beam a microwave transmission from one station to another, from one city to another, and therefore from one "switch" to another. The transmission towers were spaced about 30 miles apart. A call from New York to San Francisco went through 100 relay towers. Early microwave transmission used four channels, each with its own carrier frequency near 4 GHz. Each channel could carry one television signal or 500 telephone bands. Microwave transmission always was along line of sight. Once you found a microwave tower, you could hike to it and see the next tower somewhere on the horizon. This kind of microwave transmission worked for a few decades.

The next disruption to telecommunications technology came with Sputnik. It didn't take long to figure out that a few satellites in low earth orbit could be used as microwave relay stations. Furthermore, they could relay radio transmissions across oceans. A commercial satellite company, Comsat, was formed in the mid 1960s. By the end of the 1960s, a relatively small collection of telecomm satellites was doing a better job than the very large number of relay towers. This technology would last two or three decades before a new disruptive technological breakthrough.

First, let's get back to the local landline network. A twisted pair of copper wires can carry voltage waves for a few miles. Wherever you live, your landline phone has a dedicated line (twisted pair of wires) that goes directly to a *switch*. There is a switch within 2 or 3 miles of your phone. The switch might be in its own building. The building may be marked as phone company property. Or not. It need not have windows. In my semi-rural area, the switch is in a brick building with windows and shutters, made to look like a house. Looking closely, the windows are fake and there's a small sign on the side that identifies the building as property of the phone company. If you go inside a switch, there are thousands to tens of thousands of relays and hundreds of thousands of twisted pairs. In cities, the switch need not have its own building. It might occupy rooms in a larger structure. Every switch has a room full of large, lead-acid batteries. In case of power failure, the batteries provide the necessary voltage (about 2 V) to power the phone lines for 6 to 8 hours. Your landline phone does not operate using your power line. It has a dedicated dc voltage that comes from the phone company. That's why your phone might work during a power outage. In New York City, many of the switches in Manhattan are located in the basements of buildings. This was a problem during Hurricane Sandy. Streets and basements in lower Manhattan were flooded and the switches and emergency batteries were shorted out. It was one of the few times that landlines have been shut down completely by a natural disaster.

The early copper wire twisted pairs were not of great quality. Even so, the bandwidth was a few hundred thousand Hz (few hundred KHz). Recall that the bandwidth needed for talking is only about 6 KHz. For many years, twisted pair phone lines were equipped with a filter that allowed transmission only of low frequencies. This is called a low pass filter, and the cutoff had a knee of about 8 KHz. The purpose was to filter out high frequency noise, which sounds like hissing. So the phone company was throwing away bandwidth. They had a few hundred KHz available, but really only needed 6 KHz. So they kept about 1% of the bandwidth and threw away the rest. In the view of the phone company, there was no use for frequencies of 10 KHz to 1 MHz. With the rise of television, a few people floated the idea of picture phones that transmitted sound along with televised pictures. Black and white TV transmission required a bandwidth of around 2 MHz. This was nearly within reach, but the cost of a transceiver for pictures and sound was prohibitive. As materials and production methods improved, the bandwidth of twisted pair lines increased. At the dawn of the internet age, digital subscriber lines (DSL) used twisted pairs and had bandwidths of order 10 MHz, or even a bit more.

Optic Fiber

As early as the 1920s, scientists were working with thin glass fibers and had the idea of using a bundle of glass fibers to transmit an image. Light waves incident on one end of a single glass fiber would transmit to the other end. Transmission made use of two technical approaches. The first is the principal of "total internal reflection." Light that is travelling in glass, with a large index of refraction, reflects perfectly off a surface with air, which has a small index, if the light approaches the interface at a low angle (refer to the photograph on the cover). For a long, thin fiber, the light beam is always approaching the side surfaces at a low angle and all the reflections are perfect. The second approach was simply to make the glass more transparent by making it more pure.

The next idea would be to take a bundle of these fibers. One could focus an image onto the ends of fibers in a bundle. Each fiber would transmit incident light, from a portion of the image, from one end to the other. If the fibers kept the same order along the entire length of the bundle, then the light coming out the other ends would correspond with the incident image. This was the idea for the invention of endoscopes.[5] As is often the case with technology, success breeds more success. The success of endoscopy propelled the development of better optic fibers: better transmission (higher purity), narrower diameter, and longer length. In 1959, American Optical Company could draw a fiber with a diameter so narrow that it would transmit only a single wavelength of light. This is called a single mode fiber. Elias Snitzer (American Optical) 1961 published a paper (1961) describing this as a "single-mode optical waveguide" and including a rigorous theoretical treatment.

By the early 1960s, several groups were studying the idea of communication using optical waveguides. There were many crucial issues. A carrier radio wave is coherent; the wave starts at the transmitter and ends at the receiver. Natural light is incoherent, so a coherent light source would be needed. A second key issue is the length of transmission. There is little need to communicate from one room to a room next door. If optic waveguides were to have any practical use, an optical fiber with very high transparency was required. This characteristic can be quantified by measuring the losses. For example, you take a fiber cable that's 1000 meters (1 km) long. Pick out a light source and measure the power of the light (in watts or milli-watts). Apply the light at one end of the cable and measure the power of the light that comes out the other end. The loss is described by the ratio of detected light relative to the incident light. The ratio is measured using a logarithmic scale that has units of *decibels* (dB). A light beam ten times more powerful than a reference beam is 10 dB more powerful. A beam 100 times more powerful is 20 dB more powerful. A beam at the end of a 1 km long fiber with power that is 1/100 (1%) of the incident power is weaker by 20 dB. Another way to say this is that the beam loss is 20 dB. By the way, a *decibel* is one tenth of a *bel*. The bel was named after Alexander Bell because the term was invented by telephone technicians who were measuring transmission losses along twisted pair phone lines. This will be important in the next few paragraphs.

Many years ago, my mother became highly enamored with Corning Glass Works. They invented a kind of ceramic dish that was almost unbreakable. It was called "Corelle Dinnerware." Furthermore, the dishes and plates didn't look bad and, best of all, they were almost affordable. When you figured that they'd last forever, they were a bargain. That's all that I knew about Corning. The company is located in Corning, New York. The company has an active research laboratory, doing materials, chemistry and physics research. Who would guess that a tidal wave of innovation would begin in the small town of Corning, New York?

The real beginning was at the British Post Office Laboratories. There, in 1966, Frederick Francis Roberts began a research program in fiber-optic communications. It was obvious that the central research issue was the creation / invention of an optic fiber that had extraordinary transparency. A visiting scientist from Corning learned about the program. When he returned home, he talked with Robert Maurer and they began a very small project on fused silica (a kind of glass) fibers. A year later, the British Post Office Laboratories increased their effort on fiber optics and an unofficial race to develop low-loss (highly transparent) fiber was on. The initial goal was fiber with an attenuation of 20 dB/km. Reviewing the discussion of the earlier paragraph, this means that the power of the light at the end of a 1 km fiber would be 1% of the power that was incident at the beginning. This rather modest goal was believed to be a proof of plausibility for commercial development. At Corning, initial attempts to draw fiber went badly. Maurer persisted and he arranged for Peter Schultz, from the Chemistry Department, to join the project part time. A year later, Donald Keck became the first staff scientist to work full time on the project. By 1970 the Corning group had achieved a fiber that would transmit a single frequency of laser light (a single mode, with wavelength of 633 nm - red) with a loss of 17 dB/km. Two years later they reported measurements on a multimode fiber (it transmitted more than a single frequency) with a loss of 4 dB/km. That means that light at the end of a 1 km fiber had a power level of 40% of the light that was incident at the start! In two years they had increased the transmission by a factor of 20! In a biographical article, Keck described how he tested his fibers[6]. He would wind a long length of fiber on a spool. A laser would send light with a measured power into one end and he'd measure the power coming out the other end. After a couple of years measuring transmitted powers of roughly one percent, he was testing a sample of fiber in 1972 and looked into the end. He describes nearly being blinded. He calls this mishap his "ah – ha" moment, when he knew that Corning's research had succeeded at something that would become important. No one had any idea how important it would be.

Diode lasers

The invention and development of optic fiber is only half the story. Communication using light with fiber optic waveguides was alive in the minds of a few visionaries, but it faced a second big problem.

The standard technology used radio waves as carrier waves for communication. Different portions of the radio frequency spectrum are set aside for different kinds of communication, as regulated by the Federal Communications Commission (FCC). It works the same for radio, television, and long distance telephone. How is the carrier wave created? There is a transmitting antenna. For simplicity, think of a straight piece of metal wire that has a length matched to half the wavelength of the carrier. A voltage wave is applied to the antenna and this causes the conduction electrons in the wire to move back and forth in unison, all along the wire. The moving electrons emit radio waves. The emitted carrier wave is intrinsically coherent because the source is coherent: all the conduction electrons in the antenna move back and forth at the same time. It's one long continuous wave at a fixed frequency. The wave spreads out in the atmosphere around it, in a way similar to water waves spreading out from a float that bobs up and down at a fixed rate. The carrier wave is mixed with an information band, and you know the rest – it was described above.

On the other hand, all natural light is intrinsically incoherent. Each photon (massless particle of light) is a wave packet and not a continuous wave. The wave packet has a beginning and an end. For visible light a photon is about one meter long. Each photon comes from a unique source. Specifically, a photon in the visible range of the spectrum comes from an atom. Suppose you have a fluorescent light. The bulb is filled with a gas and a voltage is applied from one end of the tube to the other. Each atom in the gas has an electron that is excited by the voltage (equivalently stated, it makes a transition to a higher energy level) and then the atom emits a photon when the electron relaxes back to a lower energy (makes a transition to a lower level). And then the process repeats. In this way, each photon coming out of the bulb at any instant comes from a different atom. The photons don't all have the same wavelength. This is why the light is white. Usually the photons have one of 3 or 4 different wavelengths, each wavelength representing a specific transition. And furthermore the light is not coherent.

It would be impossible to use light as a carrier wave were it not for the laser. Laser light has two important properties. First, it is monochromatic (single frequency) – every photon has the exact same frequency. Second, it is coherent. Every photon of visible light is about 1 meter long. In natural light, every photon is on its own – it goes its own way. For laser light, the tip of one photon is connected to the tail of another. You end up with a single beam of light that is coherent and collinear (all the photons are going along the same path). With good lasers, the coherence can be nearly perfect and a single wave can be coherent for many km. If lasers had not been invented, no visionary would have imagined that light communication would succeed.

So what is a laser? Once again I'll give a simplified description that's approximately true. There are many different kinds of lasers but we'll talk about a solid state laser, one that uses a solid material rather than a gas. Any atom has many possible electronic energy levels and a number of common transitions between levels. I'll describe a ruby laser. This was the first kind of laser that was demonstrated.[7] A ruby crystal is aluminum oxide that's doped with a small amount of chromium. The chromium doping (doping is described further down) creates three convenient energy levels. We number them from lowest (also called the ground state) to highest as E_1, E_2 and E_3. The difference in energy between E_1 and E_2 equals the energy of a photon of red light with wavelength λ. The energy difference between E_1 and E_3 corresponds to a violet photon, which has larger energy and shorter wavelength. The energy difference between E_3 and E_2 is relatively small; the transition between these two states does not produce photons.

Take a small ruby crystal and make the length whatever you want as long as it is exactly an integer number of wavelengths of the laser light (the true requirement is an integer number of half-wavelengths, but let's overlook that detail). In other words, length L is equal to n times λ (wavelength) and n must be a round number (an integer) and not a fraction. Polish the ends and put a perfectly reflecting mirror on one end. Put another mirror, one that isn't quite perfectly reflecting, on the other end. A narrow diameter tube is wrapped around the ruby crystal. The tube is filled with xenon gas. The ruby laser has output in the form of pulses. To operate the laser, apply a high voltage pulse to the xenon in the tube. The xenon atoms make transitions that give off violet photons. This is called the *pump pulse*. As these are absorbed by the ruby crystal, electrons make a transition from E_1 to E_3. The transition from E_3 to E_2 happens quickly, but the state E_2 lasts a relatively long time. There is a typical (average) time for the electron to relax back to the ground state, a process called spontaneous emission. If the pump pulse produced a lot of excited electrons in state E_2, spontaneous emission won't be fast enough to return them to the ground state and a large fraction of the atoms will have electrons in the excited state. This is called a population inversion and it's not normal. It's called an unstable (or metastable) state because it will return to normal as quickly as possible. Now that you've created an unstable, inverted population, the appearance of one photon passing by an atom can cause an excited electron to relax and emit another photon. This is called stimulated emission. The explanation is not simple so we'll just accept that it happens. Stimulated emission is like a cascade: one photon stimulates the emission of another, giving you 2 photons. Each of these can stimulate the emission of another, giving you 4 photons. By continuing this way you get light amplification (one photon leads to the creation of many). That's the heart of a laser: Light Amplification by Stimulated Emission of Radiation (with the radiation being visible light). But remember that the ruby crystal has a length that is exactly an equal number of wavelengths. Each photon is a wave packet that's many wavelengths long (a few million). A wave is a repeating series of peaks and troughs. The midpoint between a peak and trough is called a node. Any photon that reflects off one end of the crystal at a nodal point of its waves will reflect perfectly (refer to Figure 1). Since the other end is an exact number of wavelengths away, the photon will reflect perfectly at that end as well. The photons that don't reflect perfectly are scattered and re-absorbed by the crystal and all the photons that reflect perfectly form a perfectly coherent wave, called a standing wave, inside the crystal. Finally, remember that one of the ends of the crystal is not completely reflecting. A small amount of the light will leak out through that mirror and form a highly directional (the beam doesn't spread), coherent traveling wave. Even though it's only a fraction of the laser light that leaks out, the intensity of light inside the laser is so high that the leaked laser beam is very bright.

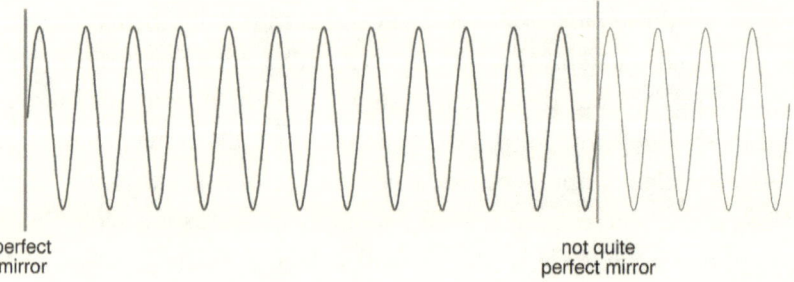

perfect
mirror

not quite
perfect mirror

Figure 1. Standing waves inside a laser. The two vertical lines represent mirrors. The left mirror is a perfect reflector and the right mirror allows a small amount of light to pass through. The length of the laser is an exact number of wavelengths of the laser light.

The first lasers were big and expensive. The ruby lasers had pulsed output with pulses lasting about 1 millisecond. The pump pulse created a population inversion. When the stimulated emission reduced the population inversion the laser pulse ended and you had to repeat the process with the next pump pulse. Lasers were soon made using a mixture of gases. These lasers had continuous output, but they still were big and expensive. An optic communication network would need lots of cheap lasers. You need a laser as a transmitter at each end of an optic waveguide. And you need more than that.

Remember what we learned a few pages back: voltage waves being transmitted along a twisted pair can travel several km before they are too weak to be received reliably. So what do you do if you have a twisted pair that must stretch for many km? What do you do when you transmit voltage pulses along lines bundled inside a trans-oceanic cable? Well, every few miles or tens of miles you have a repeater. A repeater is composed of a receiver, amplifier and transmitter. You receive the voltage waves, amplify them and transmit them again so they go further down the line. That means that the trans-oceanic cable is not just a bundle of phone lines. There is a power line to provide electricity to the amplifiers. And there are cables for structural strength.

Optic communication would work the same way. The laser light would gradually attenuate (get dim) as it is transmitted down a fiber. You install a repeater at a distance where it is still bright enough to be received reliably. In the early days the repeater would be a receiving transducer (to receive the light and transform it to a voltage), a voltage amplifier and then a transmitter that converts the voltage signal back to laser light (present technology repeaters are simpler). So every few miles or tens of miles you would need a laser. That's a lot of lasers for a trans-oceanic fiber optic line that's five or ten thousand miles long. And each repeater needs power. The early gas lasers were almost affordable, but still pretty expensive. Each was a cylinder, about the size of an automobile shock absorber, that was filled with a mixture of helium and neon, and each required relatively high power. The technology would need a small, inexpensive, low power laser that was easy to manufacture and package. That would be the diode laser.

A diode laser begins with a diode. Your typical diode is made of silicon and is called a "p-n junction diode." Pure silicon is a semiconductor that has very few carriers and conducts electricity poorly. By adding impurities (atoms other than silicon) to the silicon one can introduce carriers. The impurity is called a dopant. A donor dopant adds mobile electrons (it donates electrons) and the result is an *n-type* semiconductor. An acceptor adds mobile holes, which are positively charged carriers (it accepts, or absorbs, electrons and leaves behind a hole) and the result is called a *p-type* semiconductor.

A simple schematic picture of a *p-n* junction diode is shown in Figure 2(a). A *p-type layer* is on top, shown with cross-hatched shading. The light gray spheres depict the mobile holes. An *n-type* layer is beneath it, shaded medium gray. The dark gray spheres depict the mobile electrons. The thin, top and bottom layers (diagonal hatching) represent thin metal layers that contact the semiconductor (called electrodes) and these layers then can be attached to metal wires. The interface between the semiconducting layers is called a depletion zone (light gray). When the two layers are put together, the electrons and holes very near the interface meet each other and cancel out. The process of an electron and a hole meeting is called annihilation. After the region near the interface is depleted of most carriers, an internal electric field is established and the field keeps the carriers away from the interface region. That's why the interface region is called a depletion zone. It also is sometimes called a barrier because the lack of carriers means this region has high electrical resistance.

The *p-n* junction diode is a useful electronic device that creates a one-way street for electric current. Figure 2(b) shows the same diode with a battery attached. Here the battery applies a positive voltage to the *p* region and a negative voltage to the *n* region. This is called forward bias. The voltage creates an electric field in the diode. Electrons in the *n* region move up towards the positive voltage electrode, holes move down towards the negative voltage electrode, and an electric current is allowed to flow in this direction. A hole moving down counts the same as an electron moving up, so the total current is the sum of the electron and hole currents. What happens to the carriers? An electron crosses the barrier and doesn't go very far before it meets a hole and they annihilate. The annihilation releases energy. For silicon p-n junction diodes, the energy is pretty small and takes the form of a lattice vibration called a phonon (like a sound wave). Eventually the phonons dissipate their energy as heat. It's the same story for a hole. It doesn't go very far past the barrier before it meets an electron and annihilates.

Now suppose the battery is hooked up in the opposite direction, with a positive voltage applied to the n region and a negative voltage applied to the p region (not pictured in Figure 2). This is called reverse bias. In this case the electrons move down towards the positive voltage electrode and the holes move up towards the negative voltage electrode. In this case, the result is that a very small current flows. Here's a helpful way to think about this. With forward bias, the depletion zone becomes very narrow and the barrier (the resistance of the depletion region) is low. For reverse bias, the depletion region becomes very wide, the barrier is high and the resistance is high. For low resistance the voltage drives high current. For high resistance, the voltage drives low current.

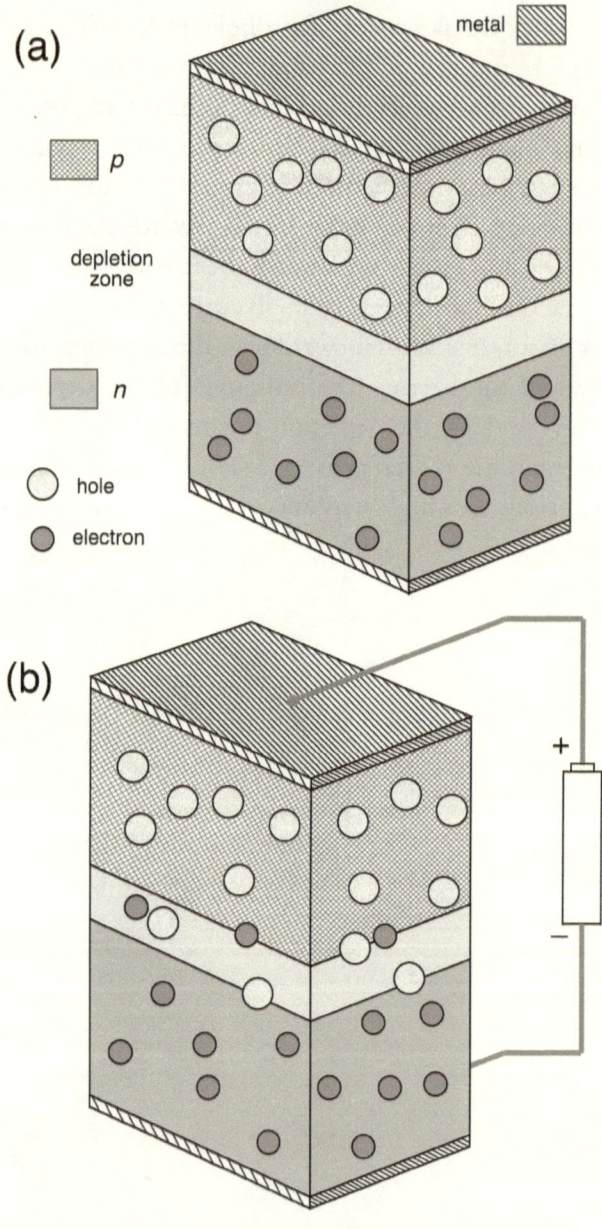

Figure 2. A schematic view of a *p-n* diode (a) in equilibrium and (b) with forward voltage bias.

So a diode is a useful device that allows current to flow for a positive voltage, but blocks a current from flowing for a negative voltage. It became much more interesting when researchers began making diodes with materials other than silicon. The energy emitted during annihilation depends on the material. For silicon, as mentioned above, the energy is pretty small. But physicists started making diodes using compound semiconductors, materials like gallium arsenide. They discovered that the energy released by annihilation was much larger. It was large enough that the energy was released as a photon of light. Thus was born the light emitting diode (LED).[8] Figure 3(a) is a schematic sketch of a *p-n* junction diode made with a compound semiconductor and under forward bias. As electrons and holes move across the barrier, they annihilate and each annihilation gives off a photon of light. The light comes out of the side of the structure. An LED might have a transverse dimension of a micron or so. It's usually packaged with reflecting surfaces around it so that the light coming out the sides is scattered in all directions. This makes the LED more easily seen. The color of the emitted light is determined by the material that's used for the diode. Gallium arsenide was originally used for red. At the present time, aluminum gallium indium phosphide (AlGaInP) alloys are used for red, orange and yellow LEDs. Small changes in the composition of the AlGaInP change the color between yellow and red. Indium gallium nitride (InGaN) alloys are used for green and blue. A blue LED can be used for white. The LED is surrounded by a phosphorescent material that absorbs blue and emits many wavelengths – therefore the light is white.

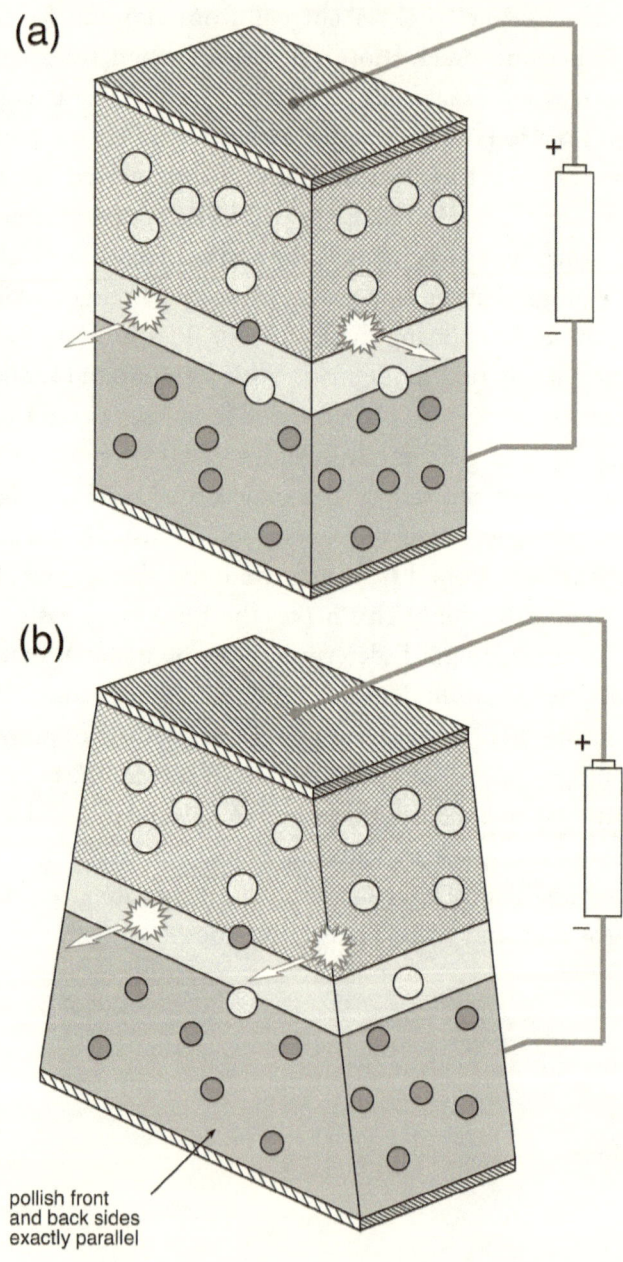

(a)

(b)

pollish front
and back sides
exactly parallel

Figure 3. A schematic view of (a) a light emitting
diode (LED) and (b) a diode laser.

Many scientists contributed to the invention and development of the LED. James R. Baird and Gary Pittman (Texas Instrument) made the first LED. It emitted infrared light with a wavelength of 900 microns. Nick Holonyak, Jr. (General Electric) developed the first LED with visible light (red) in 1962. The output power of these early LEDs was too low to be very useful. Improvements followed rapidly and costs came down quickly.

Finally we get to laser diodes. Figure 3(b) shows an LED that has some important modifications. First, the box shaped stack of layers now looks like a wedge. Two sides of the stack are tapered. The tapered angle suppresses light emission through these sides, so the photons come out either the front or back of the other sides. The two straight sides are polished, and the thickness of the wedge is set to be exactly a wavelength, or an integral number of wavelengths, of the photons that are produced by annihilation. The back surface is coated with a thin metal layer that acts as a perfectly reflecting mirror. The front surface is coated with a similar metal layer, but the reflection is not quite perfect. It lets some of the light out. Now the depletion region of the diode acts like the cavity of the ruby solid state laser that we discussed above with Figure 3. Photons that are trapped in the layer are synchronized coherently into a standing wave. The front surface lets out a fraction of the light as a coherent laser beam.

Robert N. Hall (General Electric) filed his patent for the idea of a diode laser late in 1962, and it was granted in April, 1966.[9] My simple explanation ignored details of the diode structure that encourage population inversions of electrons and holes and permit stimulated emission, and many physicists made key contributions. Herbert Kroemer (Varian Central Research Laboratory) created a structure that trapped electrons at the junction so they could more easily combine with holes and emit light. Zhores Alferov and Rudolf Kazarinov came up with a very similar idea independently, at the Ioffe Physics Institute in Russia, and later made the first structures. Kroemer and Kazarinov were awarded a Nobel prize.

The first diode lasers operated at low temperature. It would be several more years before lasers operating at room temperature were developed, and still longer before diode lasers could operate at room temperature and have a long lifetime (100 years, as measured in the lab). The diode laser is compact and inexpensive and its development was the final key to the success of fiber optic communications. Bell Labs worked on diode lasers extensively, concentrating on GaAs diodes. By the time GaAs lasers were reliable, optic fiber was being manufactured with optimal transparency in the range of infrared light, 1.3 to 1.55 microns (best for wavelength division multiplexing). J. Jim Hsieh and C. C. Shen (Lincoln Lab, MIT) had demonstrated room–temperature operation of InGaAsP lasers at 1.25 micron. The InGaAsP laser diodes were improved and used for the optic fiber network. GaAs laser diodes have been employed for other mass-market applications such as CD players and laser printers. For optic fiber, laser diodes are used at the transmission end. For many years they also were used as repeaters. At the present, the repeaters used in trans-oceanic cables are a newer invention, the Erbium Doped Fiber Amplifier.

By the early 1990s the phone company had all the pieces it needed to create a new telecommunications platform with broad bandwidth transmission and based on optic fiber. But how could they afford to replace the existing network of tens of hundreds of thousands of miles of copper wires, as well as microwave transmission stations? It would be a huge expense.

Of course, they didn't pay the huge cost of that replacement. You did. They can make the customer pay, amortized over a few years, if the regulators allow. Why would the regulators allow that? Scientists measured the decay length of a laser beam that was transmitted down an optic fiber. They compared that with the decay length of a voltage pulse applied to a twisted pair of copper wires – which was the basis of the existing network. At the time of the test, when the phone company was laying optic fiber in the early 1990s, a transmission line based on copper wires required an amplifier approximately every 3 km. A transmission line based on optic fiber required an amplifying repeater every 4 km (At the present time (2017), optic fiber is so good that the best fiber needs a repeater every 100 km). The company took these data to the regulators and argued that it was more reliable and less expensive for them to replace existing copper lines with fiber optic, compared with continuing to replace old copper lines with new copper lines. They won. In fact, they were allowed to replace old copper lines that didn't need replacing with new optic fiber. And they passed the cost right on to the consumer.

As a scientist, all of this is really quite incredible. After years in the lab, my intuition is that copper is a great conductor. After all, you can transmit a voltage wave for miles with little loss. Similarly, I think of glass as a fairly poor transmitter of light. A glass window is very clear but it's only an eighth of an inch thick. When I go to the bank I see glass (or Plexiglas) that's a few inches thick. Looking edge-on, so that I'm looking through a foot or two of glass, the image from the other side looks a bit dark and blurry. It's hard to imagine looking through a piece of glass that's many miles long and clearly seeing the light of a flashlight bulb at the other end. But optic fiber is that good. Decades of research have made the glass in optic fiber completely pure and free of defects – so much so that you could see light at the end of a 65 mile long piece of fiber. It's hard to look through 65 miles of air!

For those who ran the phone company, the dramatic increase in bandwidth was incredible. A copper coaxial cable carries millions of bits per second (several Mb/sec). A high quality optic fiber carries several trillion bits (several Tb/sec).[3] That's an improvement of a factor of a million. Within a matter of a few years, the bandwidth of transmission lines in their platform increased by 6 orders of magnitude compared with cable, and by 8 orders of magnitude compared with twisted pair.

Imagine what it was like to be the CEO of the phone company when this was happening. Here's an analogy to think about. The CEO of a major auto manufacturing company is working at his desk.

The Vice President for Research comes into his office and says "We've got a good result in the lab. You should come and see this."

The focus of research has been improving gas mileage. Most models are getting an average of 28 mpg. The CEO says:

"Did they get the mileage up to 30 or 32 mpg?"

The VP of Research says "Come down to the lab and I'll let the chief scientist tell you."

When they get to the lab, the scientist reports "We've invented an engine that gets 30 million miles to the gallon."

The CEO is incredulous at first, but gradually he comes to believe it. If you're the CEO, what will you do? How will this invention change your business?

First, you give the scientists who made the discovery a bonus. As time goes on, you realize what you really need: You need people to help you figure out new ways to use the engines that get 30 million miles to the gallon. Soon you're hiring different kinds of engineers and people with business minds to help think of new ways to exploit your break-through. After awhile it occurs to you: Why do I still need these scientists? They're still doing research on ways to improve an engine but that's nothing. I don't need them to tinker around to see if they can get 30,000,100 miles to the gallon. It will take many years to come up with ways to use this invention. I won't need these scientists for decades.

So you fire all the scientists and close down the basic research lab. That's what the phone company did.

CHAPTER

8

The Field Effect Transistor

It's commonly known that the transistor was one of the historic scientific breakthroughs of the post WW2 era, and that it was invented at Bell Labs by Walter Brattain, John Bardeen and William Shockley (BBS). Their ground-breaking experiments were performed in December 1947. The results were publicly announced in June, 1948, and they won the Nobel prize in 1956. The last chapter offered a discussion of semiconductors and how they are used in light emitting diodes and diode lasers. Now we continue the discussion of semiconductors and learn a little about transistors. The following discussion is not very detailed, but I explain what you need to know in order to look at the big picture of the role of transistors in high technology. BBS invented something now known as a bipolar transistor and it was based on the semiconducting element germanium (Ge). Bipolar transistors were a big deal because they could amplify electric current.

In the beginning, before the transistor, there was the triode. This was an early form of an electronic device. It was vacuum tube roughly the size of two fingers, and it usually had 3 electrodes. It was mostly used as an amplifier but also found use as an oscillator, a source of alternating voltage or current. It had been around since circa 1906. It was big, fragile and used a lot of power. But it enabled the first consumer electronics revolution, in the 1920s. The fraction of US GDP represented by sales of high tech products (radios, phonographs and telephones) in the 20's was about the same as the fraction of GDP spent on high tech today. The triode was used in commercial radios and televisions as late as the 1950s. If you find an old tube radio or TV, many of the glass components you find inside are triodes.

Bipolar transistors amplify electric current and they were better, smaller, more efficient, more robust and cheaper than triodes. Figure 4(a) shows a sketch of a *planar bipolar transistor*, with a perspective view and cross-section view (Figure 4(b) is discussed later, page 87). The planar design, which is easier to manufacture, came later. The early version was a point contact or *junction transistor*. Basically, they all work the same way. One end is called an *emitter* (e), the other end is called a *collector* (c), and the *base* (b) is in the middle. If you recall an earlier discussion, a pure semiconductor has very few moving charge carriers at room temperature. With only a small number of carriers available to conduct electric current, the resistance is very high. As a conductor it is certainly better than an electric insulator but nowhere near as good as a metal. Doping is the process of implanting *dopant atoms* into the semiconductor. The implanted dopant atoms become ionized and either provide extra *electrons* or absorb electrons. In the latter case you can think of the atom as providing positive carriers called *holes*.

Just like Figures 2 and 3, the gray regions are doped with electron donors and are *n-type* semiconductors. The carriers are electrons and have a negative charge. The cross-hatched region is doped with holes and is a *p-type* semiconductor. The carriers have a positive charge. The gray and cross-hatched regions conduct electric current fairly well, but not nearly as well as a metal. The key thing to understand is the following. You start by making an electric current flow from collector to emitter. You apply a voltage from one end to the other and the current that results, I_{ce}, is small. But here's the invention: If you make a small current flow from the base to the emitter, it becomes much easier to make the current flow from the collector to the emitter and the magnitude of the current I_{ce} increases. A scientist would say it this way: Biasing a small current I_{be} from base to emitter has a large effect on the current I_{ce} from collector to emitter. The ratio of I_{ce} to I_{be} is the *current gain*. The term *gain* is a measure of how much amplification a device can provide. Strictly speaking, the ratio I_{ce} / I_{be} is the gain for the *common emitter* configuration that's in Figure 4(a). Bipolar transistors have a current gain of fifty or more. That's a big deal. You can apply a bias current of 50 micro-amps and get a collector current of about 2 milli-amps.

The transistor was a great invention because it's a small device that provides current gain. Suppose you have a small current coming from the needle of an old phonograph (today it would be coming from a photo-diode in a CD player) or from the tuner of your radio. This small current has oscillations that mimic sound waves. Send this current into your transistor as I_{be} and the current I_{ce} will amplify the oscillations and will be large enough to power a speaker and your room will be filled with music or broadcast radio.

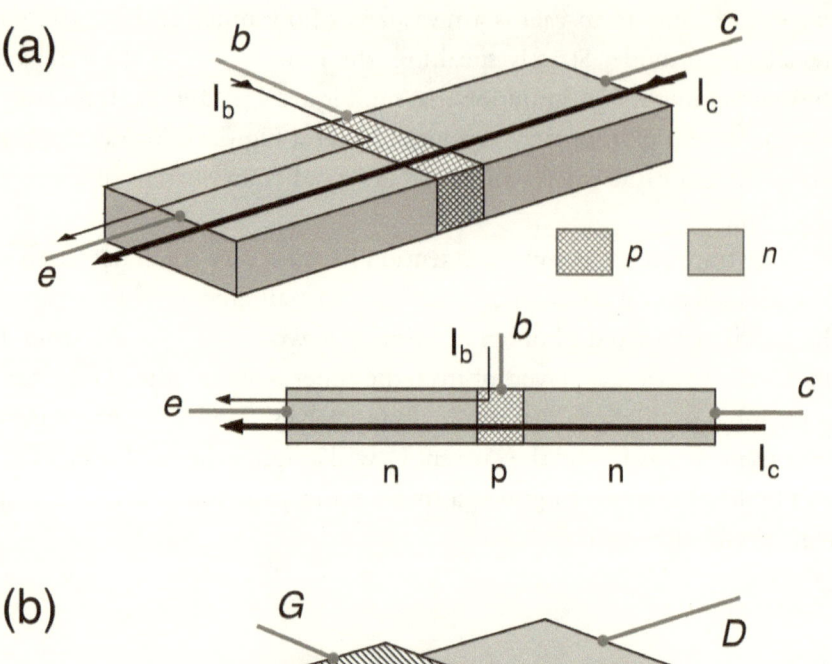

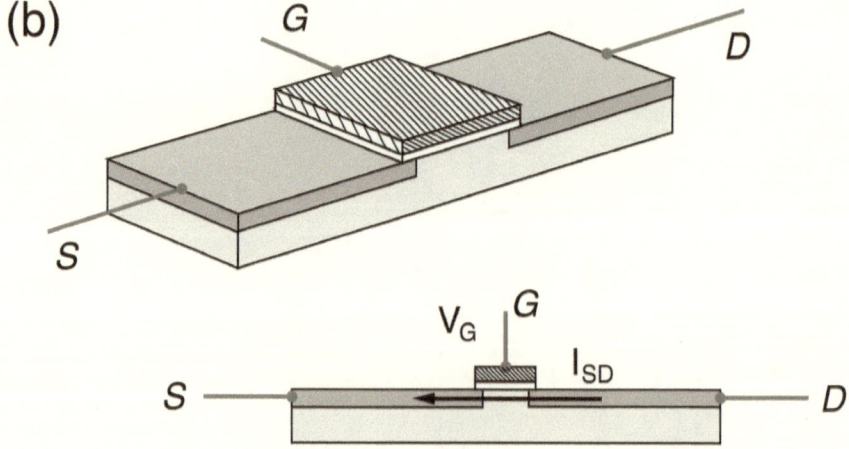

Figure 4. Perspective and cross-section sketches of (a) a planar *n-p-n* bipolar transistor and (b) a field effect transistor.

The transistor was a big deal. If you worked as an electrical engineer in the 1950s, your life and livelihood underwent major changes. In the early 1950s, you would go to the company stockroom and pick from a variety of radio tubes, each the size of a small light bulb. You'd also pick out resistors, capacitors and inductors, each the size of a coin. You would take these back to your lab bench and connect them with wires, trying to make a new circuit. Perhaps your task was to make a design that improved an existing circuit. By the mid 1960s you didn't recognize the company stockroom. The tubes were gone. They were replaced by racks with small drawers, each drawer containing a particular kind of transistor. Each transistor was the size of a pencil eraser or a bit smaller. All the circuits that used tubes were redesigned to use transistors.

After spending several years perfecting bipolar transistors at Bell, William Shockley said[1] "I'm tired of seeing my name in Physical Review Letters. I want to see it in the Wall Street Journal." He went west to California and formed a high tech startup company. The Shockley Transistor Company was founded in 1955 and was located at 391 San Antonio Rd., Mountain View. You can find the location on Google Earth using the coordinates: 37 degrees 24' 16.66" N; 122 degrees 06' 41.18" W. It is now a parking lot for a shopping center with a Safeway and a Walmart. Shockley was not a great businessman. He hired a dozen very smart people and they made transistors, one at a time. He called them his Ph. D. production line. But it didn't take long for his team to decide they didn't want to work for him.

In 1957, Gordon Moore, Robert Noyce and six others quit. Shockley later would refer to them as "the traitorous eight." They pooled $3,500 of their own money and developed a new technique for manufacturing transistors. Fairchild Camera and Instrument Corporation, a local Bay Area company, offered to invest $1.5 M in a startup venture. In October of 1957, Fairchild Semiconductor was formed.[2] And so was a business model for using venture capital in high technology.

Fairchild Semiconductor was an immediate success, exceeding anyone's imagination. Their first sale was a $15,000 order from IBM for 100 transistors. That's $150 each! But more important, Robert Noyce was working on a broader problem. He was trying to devise new techniques of manufacturing that would simplify the production of transistors, increase the output and furthermore facilitate the fabrication of circuits. In the summer of 1959, he filed a patent for the "Integrated Circuit" (IC).[3] While several scientists described ideas related to ICs, credit for the invention is given to Noyce and Jack Kilby (Texas Instruments).

It's commonly said: "Noyce and Kilby invented the computer chip." That's not quite true. They invented devices that introduced the concept of *integration*. This is such a powerful concept that it was not long before someone extended this idea to something called "Large Scale Integration" and, shortly after that, "Very Large Scale Integration" (VLSI), which is the computer chip.

Electric circuits have two kinds of components, active and passive. An active device can amplify current or voltage or power. In engineer-speak, an active device has gain (*gain* was introduced a few paragraphs above). Triodes and transistors are active devices. A passive device cannot amplify and does not have gain. Examples are resistors, capacitors and inductors. They all do something important but it would be a distraction to explain. You will find all these components if you open up an old radio or phonograph. Each component has two or three terminals. All the components are attached to a thin board punched with holes called a circuit board. Then the components are connected together by attaching wires between appropriate terminals. Noyce and Kilby both recognized that this was a problem. This was an inefficient way to make a product: gather separate components, fix them to a board, and then attach wires between each component. They both started looking for a better way. The vision was: make the board and components and wires at the same time, as a single piece. This concept became known as integration.

Noyce and others had seen parts of this vision before. We've already discussed the planar transistor. In the first generations of the transistor, separate chunks, each quite small, of bulk N and P semiconductor were joined together. Then wires were attached. The planar transistor was a big leap forward. You could take one piece of semiconductor and map out different regions – for emitter, base and collector. Then you would change the material in each mapped region and give it the characteristics you need (*n*-type or *p*-type). This was done by photolithography and ion implantation.

You start with a semiconductor wafer. A single crystal of silicon, called a *boule*, is grown from a melt. It is shaped like a long thick sausage. In those days, the diameter of the sausage was 3 or 4 inches. Today the diameter is 12 inches (0.3 meter) and a typical boule is roughly a meter long. The fact that such a large chunk of material is a single crystal is itself remarkable. It contains about 10^{27} atoms and every atom is in a perfectly registered position. Not one of the billion billion billion atoms is out of place! A diamond bladed saw cuts the boule into slices a few millimeters thick. Each slice is polished; one side is fairly rough and the other side is perfectly smooth – atomically smooth.

The basics of pattern transfer using photolithography can be described with a short description that focuses on how it's used in a silicon production line. First, photoresist (a thin photosensitive emulsion) is coated on the smooth side of the semiconductor wafer. The wafer now acts as a photographic plate. A black and white picture is projected onto the wafer, similar to the old photographic process of making a print from a negative. In this case the "negative" is called a *mask*. It's a pattern of opaque shapes that have been etched from a glass (quartz) plate coated with a metal layer – the opaque shapes are metal regions that have not been etched away. The exposure process shines ultraviolet light through the mask and onto the wafer. The wafer is then dipped in a container of a chemical developer. The developer etches away the photoresist in the regions that were exposed to light and leaves the emulsion alone everywhere else. At this point the pattern on the mask has been transferred to the wafer. And what picture is used? A picture of the circuit, or a portion of the circuit, or a device in the circuit, or a portion of a device. It's composed of simple shapes – squares, rectangles, long thin lines and such. For the planar transistor, one picture (one layer) would have two clear rectangles that show the regions mapped out to be the emitter and collector [Figure 4(a)].

For our planar transistor, we must add negatively charged carriers into the silicon in the gray regions. Suppose our first mask had two rectangles for the collector and emitter and the surface of the silicon under these two rectangles is now exposed. The carriers are added by a process called *implantation doping*. You take the wafer and put it in a big cylindrical chamber. The air is pumped out so that there is a vacuum inside, and a beam of dopant atoms is aimed at the wafer. The atoms become embedded in the silicon in the regions that are exposed. Everywhere else the atoms are embedded in the chemical emulsion and never reach the surface of the silicon. The beam is turned off, you let air back in (the vacuum is vented), the wafer is taken out and the emulsion is removed by dissolving it with another chemical. What's left is a silicon chip with two *n* doped regions [refer to Figure 4(a)]. The process is repeated for the base region. You have a different mask that has a small rectangle representing the base. You use a different beam of atoms to achieve *p* doping.

So here's the big deal – this is the equivalent of Henry Ford introducing the mass assembly line. This is an easier way to make a transistor, and to make it smaller. More importantly, you could make hundreds of these at the same time and on the same wafer (today it's billions on the same wafer). You just repeat the pattern in your "picture" hundreds of times. When you're done, you slice up the wafer into individual chips, each chip having a single transistor.

Noyce and Kilby took this vision a step further. Instead of making hundreds of identical transistors and slicing the wafer to have one transistor on each chip, why not use the wafer as the circuit board, and make all the components and wires in the circuit at the same time? There were several problems: How do you make passive components like resistors and capacitors as planar devices on a silicon surface? How do you make wires to connect them? The answer came from Kilby.

In the summer of 1958, almost everyone at the Texas Instruments Lab was on vacation. Jack Kilby was a new hire, so new that he hadn't accumulated any vacation days. He was working on the problem of making circuits smaller and easier to manufacture. One can make the N and P regions of a transistor by using photolithography and dopant implantation. Kilby reasoned that you could make a resistor in the same way. He used photolithography to pattern a long, narrow rectangle. He added carriers by implanting dopants. He could set the resistance value of his integrated semiconductor resistor by adjusting the number of dopants, or by changing the length and width of the rectangle. He made wires to connect the integrated components by the same technique. Along with resistors, he developed techniques for making capacitors and diodes and transistors. Photolithography and implantation were used to create conducting terminals for each device. Photolithography then was used to pattern paths (wires) from the terminal of one device to that of another. A high density of dopants was implanted so that these regions (wires) had a relatively high conductivity.

Kilby's specific invention was an integrated circuit for something called a *voltage controlled oscillator* (VCO). Electronic circuits are powered by direct current (*dc*); the voltages in the circuit may change levels but they do not oscillate periodically in time. Oscillating voltages and currents (also called alternating currents, *ac*) are needed for circuits used in communications or information processing, including radios and TVs (and cell phones). Vacuum tubes (triodes) were used as oscillators for decades. A VCO is a better device. It uses a transistor and creates an oscillating voltage. A dc voltage applied to the VCO can set the frequency of the oscillation. Early VCOs were the size of a breadbox, and were made using transistors and multiple passive components that were connected by soldered wires. The oscillating output could be visualized and measured by connecting the output to an oscilloscope. Kilby's integrated VCO was a small rectangle of silicon, about 11 mm on one side and two mm on the other side. The story goes that Kilby hooked up his VCO to an oscilloscope in front of a small group of engineers, in September 1958.[4] When the oscillating voltage appeared on the scope, the audience was transfixed. They couldn't believe it. If you're an engineer, this is the kind of thing you remember for the rest of your life.

The same month that Jack Kilby started work on his VCO, Robert Noyce (Fairchild Semiconductor) made notes in his lab book about integrating resistors, diodes and transistors on a single piece of silicon. The first chip that Noyce made was something called a flip-flop. This is a very basic device used to store a binary value for a short time while a logical process is going on. It's still used today. As soon as transistors were in production and became available, engineers began devising ways to use them for digital logic. Before planar transistor technology, the favored approach was called *resistor-transistor logic* (RTL).[5] A flip-flop could be made using a few transistors and resistors. Noyce made an integrated flip-flop using the resistor-transistor logic design. The key point is that he made an integrated circuit composed of several different devices, both passive and active, on a single chip. It's important that he chose a device with applications for digital signals. It's important that hundreds of these chips could be produced at once, on a single wafer, and then cleaved into individual chips. The most important thing is that the process of integration is *scalable*, a term that's very important to engineering. To summarize, Noyce and Kilby invented *integration* and showed that it works for mass producing flip-flops and VCOs. Each of these might have a dozen device components and there might be a few dozen processing steps. Examples of a processing step are applying photoresist, pattern transfer, dissolving photoresist, dopant implantation, deposition of a conducting or insulating film, etc. Integration works equally well at a much larger level. In 2017, there are many different kinds of chips, such as memory chips, microprocessors (logic chips) and communications chips. Each chip might have billions of device components and a thousand processing steps. A 12 inch wafer might be diced up to produce 1,600 chips.

I always wondered why one of the pioneer silicon electronics companies was Fairchild Camera. What prompted a camera company to invest in transistors? In those days, a camera company made most of its money from photographic films and emulsions, not lenses. Photolithography was a very clever connection to the semiconductor industry that they foresaw. Someone at Fairchild Camera in the 1950s is an unsung hero of the semiconductor revolution.

If you were an electrical engineer in the early 1970's, your life was again completely changed. The company stockroom was completely different. There still were cabinets with cubbies and racks and trays of different kinds of transistors. Now there also were cabinets with racks and trays full of ICs. There were ICs of all different kinds. VCOs, flip-flops, and Boolean logic gates (described below). Each IC was a thin rectangle about a cm long and a few mm wide. It was part of a *package* that had short metal legs along each long side, on the bottom. These legs were the terminals. They would plug into special receptacles. The receptacles could be mounted on circuit boards and wired together.

An engineer would design a circuit at his desk. He/she would go to the stock room and pick out the chips he/she needed. He/she would go to the lab bench, wire up the chips, then connect a dc power supply along with a switch. He/she would turn on an oscilloscope and apply the probes of the scope to various points in the circuit. He/she would turn the switch on and see if it worked.

Not only could you make hundreds of ICs at once on a single wafer, but also you had the possibility of making thousands at once. All you had to do was change the scale of your picture. Keep the same pictures used for the masks for each of the process levels, but shrink each picture down by the same scale to a smaller size. Now you could fit more chips onto the same wafer. Manufacturing becomes easier and the chips become cheaper. Or, you could put more devices into each IC, so that new ICs could have more complex and powerful capabilities. This happened immediately. In 1963 the average price of a chip, a simple VCO or logic gate, was $32. By 1965 a similar chip was $8. In 2000 a chip with many transistors and complex circuits was $0.05.

Engineers immediately began designing more and more complicated circuits, with a focus on information processing. The concepts that underpin the performance of mathematical logic operations using binary numbers, *digital logic*, had been around for a century. George Boole devised rules for basic binary logic steps in the 1860s. He delineated the rules of specific binary operations including AND, OR, NAND and NOR (two other important operations are called XOR and XNOR). To this day, these fundamental processes are called *Boolean logic*. You don't need to know how any of these operations work. The important thing to know is that combinations of Boolean gates can be used to add binary numbers, and any number can be represented as a binary. Furthermore, variations of these combinations can be used to multiply, subtract and divide numbers. Other combinations can be used for other logic operations such as comparison; is this number equal to that? Is it Larger?

Theorists John von Neumann and Alan Turing formulated the groundwork for digital computation in the 1930s and 40s. Alan Turing, famous as a code-breaker in World War 2,[6] was equally famous for inventing the *Turing machine*.[7] Initially, the Turing machine was a hypothetical device that could perform rudimentary operations on binary numbers. Turing made the bold assertion that this simple machine could perform any mathematical computation regardless of complexity, under the condition that it be given appropriately programmed instructions. Turing led the team that built an electrical / mechanical embodiment of such a machine. Turing's vision was quite radical at the time, but his Turing machine became the model for digital information processing that would be used for the next 80 years. It's the model still used today and likely to remain dominant for several more decades. The basic idea must be recognized as a stunning success.

The Turing machine is a *serial* (or *sequence*) *logical processor.* A string of bits (binary values) passes through the machine. The *operator* (a part of the machine that Turing called the *machine head*) performs a logical operation on a single bit and then gives instruction for the movement of the string. The string can stay in the same place; move one bit forward or one bit backwards. But the machine head operates on one single bit at a time. In the next sequence of time it operates on another bit. The most sophisticated logic chips today operate the same way. They perform an operation on a single bit in a stream of bits. In the next clock cycle they perform an operation on the next bit in the stream.[8] The first computer built by Turing may have required a fraction of a second (a tenth or hundredth of a second) for each step. Processors today operate with clock cycles on the order of one nanosecond.

Returning to the historical discussion, both von Neumann and Turing foresaw that a computer should comprise four basic functions: 1) input (to take in data and instructions), 2) memory (to store data and instructions), 3) process (to perform the calculations), 4) output (to report the answer). At the time, there were computation machines that were built to perform a specific calculation, such as calculations of the trajectories of projectiles like artillery shells. The broader concept of Von Neumann and Turing was quite new. Their concepts are considered "high level" viewpoints – an examination that's an overview of a whole system. American Claude Shannon (Bell Labs) contributed the opposite perspective of digital processing ideas, a "low level" approach. He proposed ways to design and fabricate the building blocks of a computer, specifically binary Boolean logic gates. One of his papers, before transistors were invented, proposed specific designs for AND and OR gates that could be made using electromagnetic relay switches.

Engineering work in the area of digital logic was active in the 1950s and 60s and then accelerated with the inventions of the transistor and IC. In 1960, Fairchild marketed several different ICs called *micrologic elements*. Each was a digital logic gate composed of 3 or 4 transistors plus several diodes and resistors. Each was priced at about $120. The cost, much higher than an equivalent gate built on a circuit board using separate components and wires, priced the technology out of reach for consumers. Unless you were the US government.

Also in 1960, President Kennedy announced the Apollo moon program. In a speech at Rice University, Sept. 12, 1962, President Kennedy said:[9] "...Surely the opening vistas of space promise high costs and hardships, as well as high reward.... our leadership in science and in industry, our hopes for peace and security, our obligations to ourselves as well as others, all require us to make this effort... and to become the world's leading space-faring nation.... We set sail on this new sea because there is new knowledge to be gained, and new rights to be won, and they must be won and used for the progress of all people.... We choose to go to the moon in this decade and do the other things, not because they are easy, but because they are hard...."

Kennedy was an inspiring president and his proposal to go to the moon was, politically, a very successful idea. It also was crucially important to the young electronics industry. Money for the program was not an obstacle. Fairchild's chips were ideal for missiles and aerospace. They could be used for Guidance and Navigation. They were small, light weight, reliable, and used relatively low power. NASA launched a satellite in 1963, called IMP, that was the first to have a chip that was used for guidance. In the year 1963, a half million ICs were sold to the government. In fact, the US government bought approximately 100% of all chips sold until 1964.[10] By 1969, the Apollo program alone had purchased more than 1 million ICs. The first chip to be sold in the public commercial market was in 1964. The amplifier chip, the same IC that was in the IMP satellite, was used in a Zenith hearing aid.

In 1968, Noyce, Moore and Andy Grove left Fairchild. One plausible story is that they were upset that Fairchild passed up Noyce for promotion to CEO. They left with the goal of starting a company that would concentrate on memory chips. They were helped by venture capitalist Arthur Rock. He put up $10K of his own money, raised $2.5M elsewhere, and became the first Chairman.[11] The company, originally called "NM Electronics" for Noyce and Moore, decided a better name was Intel – a contraction for Integrated Electronics. The dominant memory technology in the market was *magnetic core*, which used tiny toroidal (ring-shaped) electromagnets, and typical memories could store several thousand bits. Intel's first memory was a 1 Kilobit (Kb) random access memory (RAM). In 1973 they manufactured a 4 Kb RAM. Sales that year were $60 M.[12] It's worth noting that there are 8 bits per byte and a 4 kilobit (Kb) chip is also denoted as a 0.5 kilobyte (KB) chip. At the present time (2017), 1 Gb memory chips are in production. Typically these RAMs are sold with configurations of 4, 8 or 16 chips grouped together in one unit (4, 8 or 16 Gb memories). The increase in bit-count is a factor of 250,000 in 44 years for this particular example. The bit-count doubled about 18 times in 44 years, or about once every 2.4 years. There are various statements of Moore's law, but a doubling time of 2 years is often given.

In 1971, the first successful consumer product to use ICs was introduced: the *pocket calculator*. It didn't really fit in your pocket. It weighed 2.5 pounds and sold for $150. But it sold like crazy. The calculator became the breakout product for the industry. At first, the functions of input, memory, processing (calculating) and output were performed by separate ICs. The next technology leap came soon: All the circuitry for the calculator's logic operations was put on a single chip. This kind chip became known as a *Microprocessing Unit* (MPU), or *Microprocessor*. Intel marketed an MPU (the 4004 IC) in 1971 for $200 and called it a computer on a chip. The generic name would later change to *Central Processing Unit* (CPU).

Looking at the technology from a low level, resistor-transistor logic was widely used when transistors were individually made. Each transistor was a small cylindrical can that stood on three stiff wire legs. With integration and planar bipolar transistors, several approaches to transistor based Boolean logic competed. IBM used their own technology, called Solid Logic Technology (SLT), for their *System 360* computer (1964). This approach had transistor chips and separate passive devices mounted on a ceramic piece. It did not become popular outside of IBM. Another approach used diodes and transistors, diode transistor logic (DTL). The design that rose to the top was called *transistor-transistor logic (TTL)*. Engineers at Fairchild were discussing ideas for transistor-transistor logic in the early 1960s, and one of their first papers came out in 1962.[13] By 1963 TTL chips had been introduced into products. Sylvania made a chip that was used in the on-board computer used for guidance in a missile that Hughes Aircraft built for the government. Texas Instruments, Motorola and others were making TTL chips by 1966. TTL had risen to dominate the market for logic chips by 1975, with a 50% market share and about $0.75 B of sales.[14] The technology wouldn't last long.

Because there was a better idea. It's something called the *Field Effect Transistor (FET)*. The original idea for the FET was by Julius Edgar Lilienfeld in 1925. He invented it to be a replacement for the triode. The idea was largely dormant for 3 decades. There was renewed interest in the late 1950s. Dawon Kahng and Martin M. Atalla, at Bell Labs, invented a silicon version of the FET in 1959.[15]

Figure 4(b) shows a FET with perspective and cross-section views. There are libraries filled with books about the details of FETs. The purpose of this discussion is to give you a simple idea of how the device works and the following description is only approximately correct. The light gray region represents the undoped silicon wafer. As before, the medium gray regions have been doped and have enough mobile electrons that these regions conduct electric current reasonable well. These two gray regions are called the *source* (S) and *drain* (D). The area with diagonal hatching represents a thin metal film, and it's separated from the surface of the device by a thin film that is electrically insulating (white). The two layers, white and hatched, form a portion of the device called the gate (G). The light gray region underneath the gate and between the source and drain is the *channel*. The material in the channel has very few mobile carriers, the resistance between source and drain is very high, and applying a voltage (V_{SD}) between source and drain will fail to cause significant current to flow. In other words, the FET is OFF when no gate voltage is applied. When you apply a voltage (V_G) to the gate, no current goes from gate to channel because the insulating barrier prevents current flow. But the voltage creates an electric field in the channel, and that field draws a few charge carriers to the surface, near the insulator. When these carriers are present, the voltage V_{SD} creates a small current from source to drain and the FET is in the ON state.

In standard practice for logic circuits, the FET operates as a very efficient voltage switch in which the current is always small; it varies from small down to very close to zero. The ratio of the amount of current that can be conducted when the switch is ON (gate voltage applied) to the amount of conducted current when the switch is OFF (no gate voltage) is the *conductance gain*.[16] FETs have gains in the range of 100 thousand to 100 million! That's a lot, and it's a lot more than bipolar transistors, with a gain of about 100. It means that you get either a little bit of current or almost zero current. The standard way to use it is as a voltage switch. In this operation mode there is very little voltage difference between source and drain when the switch is ON because a small current will flow and equalize any possible voltage difference. But if you apply a voltage (V_{DD}) to one side of the switch when it is OFF, and no voltage applied to the other side, that voltage difference will be preserved with high accuracy.

The invention of the silicon FET quickly led to the application of FETs for digital semiconductor logic, which is generically known as *CMOS*. *MOS* stands for *metal − oxide − semiconductor*, where the metal is usually aluminum, the oxide is silicon oxide, and the semiconductor is silicon. A few years after the semiconductor industry started using MOS technology, an improved version called *Complementary MOS* (*CMOS*) was developed. Many details have been swept under the rug but a few facts should be stated. Often the material in the channel is doped. For example, when the substrate is p-doped, the source and drain are n-doped and a positive gate voltage drives holes out of the channel region thereby creating a *pseudo n-type channel*. This is called an *n-MOS* device. The FET described above and depicted in Fig. 4(b) is, strictly speaking, an *enhancement mode n-MOS* FET. The opposite scheme is a *p-MOS* device. An *enhancement mode p-MOS* device is OFF for zero gate voltage and turns ON when a negative voltage is applied to the gate. There are also *depletion mode* FETS, and some FETs are in the ON state with zero gate voltage and in the OFF state when a gate voltage is applied. CMOS based logic uses both kinds of devices and that's why it's called Complementary MOS. Of course, the effect of the gate voltage can be quite different for different values of voltage and the simple discussion above emphasizes the idea of a switch that is either ON or OFF, conducting or not conducting. Having said all this, the description has been technically correct. The channel need not be doped. An FET can operate with *intrinsic* (undoped) *silicon*. This turns out to be important for scaling.

Why is the FET better than a bipolar transistor? Electric power (P) is the product of current (I) and voltage (V), P = I times V. Integrated circuits have a lot of devices and they are densely packed. Every semiconductor has a property called its *band gap* and the magnitude is a few volts. This determines the approximate operating voltage for a semiconducting transistor. The power consumed by a chip is the sum of the power consumed by all the devices and each device must operate at a few V. It follows that the best way to minimize the power used by a chip is to keep the current low. Why is it so important to keep the power low? Low power conserves electricity and preserves battery life. But by far the big problem is that the power used by the chip ends up as heat. As the chip gets hotter, the number of mobile charge carriers increases and that's bad because it's the balance of positive and negative charge carriers that makes the transistor work. As that balance changes, the gain decreases and, at high enough temperature, the transistor doesn't work any more. This creates a big problem for TTL logic. Bipolar transistors used as switches operate with high current and therefore high power.

CMOS logic dissipates power on the order of 10 nW per gate, with propagation delays of 20 to 50 nsec. TTL logic dissipates power on the order of 10 mW per gate, with propagation delays of 10 to 20 nsec.[17] CMOS power dissipation per gate is smaller than that of TTL by a factor of a million (six orders of magnitude)! This low power has enabled the development of *Large Scale Integration* (*LSI*) and *Very Large Scale Integration* (*VLSI*), which led directly to the success of Moore's law and the development of the sophisticated chips we have today – with complexity that's approximately infinitely greater than the chips of the 1970s. As of 2016, a single processor chip (CPU) can have 10 billion transistors.[18] A graphical processing chip has 16 billion transistors. This is about a billion times more complex than the first ICs. Bipolar transistor based logic could never have done this. The high power would have limited the number of devices on the chip to a number in the thousands. CMOS became the dominant digital semiconductor technology in the mid-1980s and it never has looked back. Furthermore, there are no competitors on the horizon.[19]

So the invention and development of the silicon FET and CMOS logic was a very big deal. As a switching device used in information processing, the power per device went down by a factor of about a million. And the gain of each device went up by a factor of about a million. This development happened at roughly the same time that fiber optic increased the bandwidth of communications lines by a factor of a million or more. These are classic examples of disruptive technology. They changed the world within a few years.

In an earlier paragraph, I remarked that digital logical processors use the Turing model of serial processing, more commonly called the *von Neumann architecture*. The processor performs a logical operation on one bit and then, in the next clock cycle, performs an operation on the next bit. As a brief digression, there are other ways to perform logical operations. A single string (or stream) of bits is a convenient way to store and represent data, and instructions can be stored and represented the same way. Let's suppose the digital picture of your family that's stored on your computer disk used a camera with 8 million pixels (8 MP). The image is made up of 2300 rows of 3450 pixels. Standard RGB color requires 24 bits for each pixel. Without file compression the raw file is about 192 million bits (24 million bytes). File compression, such as JPEG, reduces the file size to about 32 million bits (32 Mb) or 4 megaBytes (4 MB). That file is essentially a single stream of 32 million bits. The string includes bits that instruct the CPU (or graphical processor) when one row of pixels stops and the next begins. The string might be broken into several pieces for convenience of storage, in which case some of the bits tell the processor where, in memory, to look for the different portions of the string. By contrast, the human brain is not a serial processor. The connection between neurons is called a synapse. Any neuron might connect to more than one other neuron. Information is stored as a collection of synapses. A three pound human brain contains 0.2 trillion neurons and 125 trillion synapses. Broadly speaking, this kind of storage and processing of data is known as *parallel processing*. Rather than a sequential string of bits, data take the form of a set of bits. The picture of your family that you hold in your memory is a pattern of the states of a set of synapses. A processor that operates simultaneously on a set of bits is called a parallel processor. Models for the kind of logical operations performed by human brains are called neural networks. The first such model is almost as old as the Turing machine.[20] Warren McCulloch and Walter Pitts wrote an article about neurons and made a simple neural network model with electrical circuits (1943). Neural network research is focused on the concept of adaptive learning, meaning a circuit that can learn from the results of previous operations, but also includes ideas of parallel processing. Research on neural networks has persisted and a few circuits are used for real applications. The overwhelming success of digital information processing using the von Neumann architecture has discouraged the prospects for neural networks, and also has discouraged research on parallel processing. The ultimate parallel processor, the *quantum computer*, will be mentioned briefly in a later chapter.

It took several years before it was clear that the MOSFET would become the dominant device. But we can imagine a visit to the office of another CEO. It's the early 1980s and we visit the CEO of Big Semiconductor Company. The Vice President of Research steps into the CEO's office and says "There's something down in the lab that you really should see."

The CEO looks up and says "Why don't you just summarize it for me. Cut to the chase."

"That's hard to do. You really should see this."

They go down to the lab and talk with some of the scientists. The head of transistor research says: "We've been studying field effect transistors, also called FETs. We've been comparing them with the planar transistors used in TTL logic. The FET in CMOS logic dissipates 10 nanoWatts of power. The planar transistor in a TTL chip dissipates 10 milliWatts of power."

The CEO says "Huh? Say that again"

"The FET in CMOS logic dissipates 10 nanoWatts of power. The planar transistor in a TTL chip dissipates 10 milliWatts of power. The FET dissipates less power by a factor of a million."

The CEO looks at the VP of Research and says "Are you sure this is true?"

"Yes. We've checked the results many times. Furthermore, the MOSFET is easier to fabricate and scales more readily to smaller sizes."

The CEO goes back to his office and thinks about all this over the course of months. What will he decide to do? The first thing he does is give a bonus to the scientists involved in the research. The next thing he figures out is that his company needs engineers to design new circuits that will use all these transistors. He also needs businessmen/businesswomen who are trained to think of new products. After some time, he realizes that he doesn't really need his scientists. They did a great job, but he's got more transistors than he knows what to do with. Why should he pay for research on making an even better transistor. So he fires his scientists and shuts down the basic research division.

Finally, I end this chapter by coming full cycle and asking "What happened to Shockley, the man who arguably started it all?" He was frustrated by his lack of business success, but he took an endowed Chair as a Professor at Stanford. He lived a comfortable life and became famous, as well as reviled, for espousing racist and eugenic opinions.

CHAPTER

9

Mobile Phones to Cell Phones

Optic fiber, *diode lasers* and the *field effect transistor* were transformative inventions that were the building blocks of the physical platform that supports the information processing revolution. We can think of information as being created everywhere, then stored and processed in computers. The optic fiber forms the "trunk" lines that carry huge amounts of information between computers, servers, data storage centers and transmission towers. The user who receives and sends information is at the periphery of the system. A key technology that's changed the way the user accesses information is the cell phone and the cell network. These technologies deserve a brief description.

Mobile phones have been around for a long time, and the transition from mobile phone to cell phone was a key for information technology. Let's start at the beginning. Most people believe that the inventor of radio was Guglielmo Marconi. That's mostly true. Marconi demonstrated many of the first transmissions and receptions of radio waves, but he was broadcasting Morse Code. He was not broadcasting human voices. Some of his first broadcasts were in 1895 with a range of about 2 miles. In 1897 he broadcast a signal across the English Channel, a distance of 21 miles. He received his patent for "tuned telegraphy" a year later. In 1909 Marconi was awarded the Nobel Prize together with Karl Ferdinand Braun of Germany. Braun added improvements to Marconi's inventions. The conventional wisdom in 1900 was that radio transmission would only work along line of sight, which would be a severe limitation to its utility. In December of 1921, Marconi successfully broadcast the Morse Code for the letter "s" from Cornwall, in southwestern England, to a receiving station at Signal Hill, overlooking St. John's harbor in Newfoundland, Canada.

In the late 1880s, Heinrich Hertz had proven Maxwell's theories correct by creating and detecting radio waves in his laboratory. Research on radio was a popular topic around the turn of the century. One of the lesser known leaders in the field was a Canadian, Reginald Fessenden.[1] Early in his career, Fessenden worked for Edison, in Edison's lab in West Orange, NJ. He left at a time when Edison's funding was low and went to work for George Westinghouse. He later took a faculty position at Purdue and then moved to Western University of Pennsylvania (later renamed the University of Pittsburgh). He started working for the US Weather Bureau in 1900. They built a lab for him on an island in the Potomac River, about 45 miles southeast of Washington DC. His lab included a transmitting tower. A smaller lab, with a receiver and small transmitting tower, was built a few miles away. In December of that year. Fessenden became the first person to transmit a human voice via radio waves. He wired a microphone into his transmitter and sent a message asking his assistant if it was snowing at the smaller lab. The assistant responded with a Morse Code transmission (yes, it was snowing). He would later say that Fessenden's voice came through quite clearly in spite of randomly static noise. This work would herald the coming era of broadcast radio. It also provided the foundation for cell phones and cell networks – but that would take decades before it could be realized. For the cognoscenti, Fassenden also invented the idea for heterodyne radio receivers. His idea came 10 years before tube amplifiers, which would enable constructing the receivers, were available. He was no longer doing radio research by that time.

In 1947, a Bell Labs engineer, William Rae Young, proposed that radio towers arranged in a hexagonal pattern could support a telephone network for mobile callers. His proposal included an idea for "handoff," the technique for maintaining a transmission when the mobile caller moves from the receiving area of one tower to another. About twenty years later, Bell Labs engineers Richard H. Frenkiel and Joel S. Engel developed the technology that would support Young's design as a cellular network. AT&T sought permission from the Federal Communications Commission (FCC) to develop a commercial cellular network in the early 1970s.

The main competition with AT&T was Motorola. Bell had been concentrating on the cell network. Their research on mobile transceivers centered on car phones. Motorola was working on a truly mobile phone – one that could be carried around on the streets and in buildings. Martin Cooper led the team that designed the first practical cell phone. It was called the Motorola DynaTAC 8000x and it was not a small device. It was 9 inches long and weighed 2.5 pounds. The battery took 10 hours to charge and a charge lasted 30 minutes. Cooper was walking on the streets of Manhattan on April 3, 1973, when he made the first cell call from a prototype DynaTAC. He called Joel Engel who was, by then, the head of the cellular phone research division at Bell. Cooper reported later that Engel was surprised and the conversation was a bit stilted. Cooper's DynaTAC went on sale in 1983 at a price of $4,000 (in 1983 dollars, $9,900 in 2017 dollars).

Years ago I spoke with an elderly acquaintance who had been a young man in the early part of the twentieth century. I asked him to name the invention with the biggest impact on his life. He answered that it was the telephone. When he was young, in the 1920s, phones were still relatively uncommon. He said that the idea of talking to someone who was not in front of you was unthinkable. And to talk with someone who was a hundred miles away, or a thousand miles away, was simply unreal. I think cell phones had the same kind of impact. In the 1980s, the idea of carrying a telephone around with you and being able to call anyone at any time and from anyplace was equally unthinkable.

There were 2.4 million telephones in service in 1902. The number was 8.7 million in 1912. By 1917 the number had grown to 14.3 million (which represented 130 phones per 1,000 population).[2] The number of phones grew by a factor of 6 in the fifteen years that started in 1902.

This represented pretty fast growth considering that a phone line had to be strung from a switch to any new subscriber. That's expensive and takes time. Cell phone growth was explosively fast. At the end of 1985 there were 0.34 million subscribers in the US. The number quadrupled in 2 years; 1.2 million subscribers in 1987. Examples of the growth are found in the following subscription numbers: 5.3 million in 1990; 33.7 million in 1995; 109.5 million in 2000; 207.9 million in 2005; 300.5 million in 2010; 395.5 million in 2015. From 1990 to 2005 the number of subscribers increased by a factor of 42 (over fifteen years).[3] Such explosive growth made a lot of money for a lot of suppliers. The Nokia 1100, introduced in 2003 and discontinued in 2009, sold 250 million units worldwide.

The first cellular system widely deployed in North America used analog technology. It was called the Advanced Mobile Phone System (AMPS) and entered service in 1983. Digital technology came with the *second generation* (2G) network in the 1990s. Voices came through with more clarity, but the significance was the transition from analog to digital. The latter had many more capabilities, and the major improvement of each succeeding generation (3G, 4G) was greater bandwidth for more things – messages, internet access and streaming, and video transmission. Furthermore, digital technology allowed handsets to be smaller, less expensive, and use less power. All of these attributes added more fuel to the rocketing growth.

The inventions described in the previous few chapters, optic fiber, diode lasers and the field effect transistor, are examples of a model of creativity in which a handful of people originate and develop an innovation that had great impact. The cell phone represents a very different model, one based on incremental improvement. There are many different parts and many different chips that make up a cell phone. A few people (Steve Jobs, for example) may have had a vision for the best way to combine the parts into a product. But as an example of the incremental nature of the process, there are about 250,000 patents behind the cell phone in your pocket.[4]

CHAPTER

10

Software Overtakes Hardware

The story of Bill Gates and the birth of Microsoft has been told and retold in the geek world. Really, it helps to start the story a bit earlier. In the beginning there was IBM. Of course, the true beginning of computers was earlier, as mentioned in an earlier chapter, with pioneers such as von Neumann and Turing. But the computer revolution was all about making the computer useful and available to the average person. By the 1950s, IBM was making large computers for business and government. In 1964, IBM announced its new main frame: the *System/360*. Deliveries began a year later. Within a few years the IBM S/360 had revolutionized the main frame computer market. The S/360 was mass manufactured, adaptable to different needs and applications, and relatively inexpensive. Before this, computers were so big and specialized that each one occupied a large room and required a team of dedicated specialists to keep it running. They had been confined to universities and government laboratories and agencies. The IBM 360 could fit in a small room and could be operated by one or two technicians. The S/360 moved computers into the much larger corporate sector. It completely dominated the market. Within a few years, the S/360 was so dominant that the US government began an antitrust suit against IBM. IBM had a virtual monopoly. It was Big Blue. Big Blue's few competitors were known as *the dwarfs*.

In the mid 1970s, small, "toy" computers were introduced for small businesses and home hobbyists.[1] These were sold as kits with "some assembly required." The Altair 8800 came out in 1975. It was an immediate success but the small company, Micro Instrumentation and Telemetry System (MITS), fell apart within a few years. There were a handful of others, for example the Commodore PET and the Apple II. In 1977, Radio Shack introduced a fully assembled home computer, the "TRS-80." This desktop had a keyboard and a black and white monitor and sold for $600. It came with two games, blackjack and backgammon, and three programs (payroll, personal finance and math education) that ran from a cassette tape that plugged into a tape drive. It also came with the ability for the user to write programs. It had a compiler for BASIC[2] and included an instruction manual so that buyers could "have fun" by programing their own computer. For several years the Radio Shack desktop was the top seller, surpassing the Apple II which, in turn, surpassed the Commodore PET.

Meanwhile, back at IBM, management could not understand the interest in toy computers. In 1980 they decided it might be more than a fad and that IBM might be missing out on a product and market that they rightfully should own. IBM started a new division dedicated to this new market, the Entry Systems Division, in Boca Raton, Florida. Don Estridge was the director and Lewis Eggebrecht was the chief designer. The group was given the task to design a "personal computer" with a deadline of reaching market within a year. Estridge decided to design the computer using generic components that were widely available from a number of manufacturers and vendors. IBM designed and manufactured parts for their computers. But Estridge decided *not to use* IBM's own parts. For example, they chose to build the computer around the Intel 8088 microprocessor rather than an IBM chip. In geek talk this is called choosing an "open architecture." This would turn out to be the second worst decision ever made in the history of business. Perhaps they failed to foresee how successful a "personal" computer (small enough to fit on a desktop) would become. They also failed to foresee how successful the entire micro-computer industry would become. But once demand exploded, a dozen entrepreneurs had the same realization: they could use the same generic parts to assemble and market a clone computer with equal or better performance and a much lower price. IBM would be shut out of the personal computer market within a few years.

The IBM group made a similar decision about the software, and this would be the number one worst decision ever made. At the simplest, lowest level of operation, computers use binary signals for everything. Instructions are coded as strings of binary information (bits) that tell the processor when to read a string of input, what to do with it, and where to send the results. Similar binary codes are used to instruct the keyboard where to send input or to instruct the monitor how and when to display a string of output. At a slightly higher level, instructions that are more easily understood by humans (for example, instructions written with words and numbers) are needed to translate the workings of human logic to *machine* code. Such a program (also called code) is called an *operating system* (OS). As well as governing the basic ways the computer operates (input, output, storage, information processing), the OS can interpret a separate set of instructions (*program*) and pass them on as specific directions to the computer. The separate program is the software that makes the computer useful, such as word processors, business programs (spreadsheets), image processing, communications through the web, etc. IBM was the world leader in software. They wrote the programs for main frame computers (like the S/360) that dominated math and science (BASIC and Fortran) and business applications (COBOL). But IBM decided not to write the basic software for the personal computer project. Like buying the hardware components from outside sources, they would buy the OS externally. I reiterate the statement at the beginning of this paragraph: This would be the worst business decision ever made.

Bill Gates and Paul Allen founded Microsoft (first called Micro-Soft) in the spring of 1975. They were writing software for hobbyists – the geeks who were buying the computer kits mentioned above. Their popular product was a version of BASIC. BASIC is an acronym for *Beginner's All-Purpose Symbolic Instruction Code*. It was originally written by John G. Kemeny and Thomas E. Kurtz (Dartmouth College) in 1964. For two decades it was the basic programming language widely used in mainframes and highly popular with programmers. Allen was impressed with the introduction of the Altair 8800. He contacted the company that made it (Micro Instrumentation and Telemetry System) and discussed their need for software. Gates and Allen then moved to Albuquerque to be near the headquarters of MITS. In a matter of weeks (about 8) they wrote a version of BASIC that ran on the Altair and signed an agreement with MITS for their program to be included with each Altair when it was sold. One must admit it was a rather gutsy move by Gates and Allen to leave Harvard and Honeywell, respectively, and start a rather risky company that wrote software for a micro-computer industry that was barely viable. Gates was from a wealthy family and that made it easier to strike out on his own. Microsoft added a small number of personnel over the next few years and wrote programs for COBOL, Fortran and Pascal that would run on micro-computers. By 1980, MITS had disbanded and Microsoft had moved to Redmond, WA, and was recognized as the largest provider of standard programs for micro-computers.

The leading vendor for operating system software was Digital Research Inc. (DRI). Their operating system, Control Program for Microcomputers (CP/M), was written by the company founder, Gary Kildall. It was designed to run on any computer that used an 8-bit Central Processing Unit (CPU). The most prevalent such CPU was the Intel 8080, which was used by several of the popular home computers such as the Osborne 1 and Kaypro 2.

In the summer of 1980, IBM started discussions with Microsoft about licensing BASIC and, possibly, other programs. Microsoft had become known as a primary source for microcomputer software and had sold hundreds of thousands of licenses, a substantial number back then. It may be of equal importance that the wife of IBM CEO John Opel was a social friend of Mary Gates, the mother of Bill. It is said that Opel referred to Microsoft as the company that belonged to "Mary Gates' boy."

During their discussions, IBM also asked Microsoft for advice about the operating system. As the story goes, Bill Gates mentioned CP/M and referred them to Digital Research. He even phoned Gary Kildall personally and arranged a meeting between IBM and DRI for the next day. Kildall wasn't present for the meeting and IBM met with his wife, Dorothy McEwen, who was a DRI executive. However, IBM didn't get past the front door, both literally and figuratively.[3] The IBM team had carried their standard non-disclosure agreement and presented it to McEwen. She refused to sign it. This was only the first obstacle. The larger issue was that DRI was not convinced it would be profitable for them to make the modifications to CP/M that the IBM personal computer project needed. Specifically, IBM was using an Intel 8086 chip as the CPU for its personal computer. The 8086 was a 16-bit processor. This was a significant step up. As mentioned above, most toy computers at the time used the Intel 8080 chip, an 8-bit processor. The operating system would have to be rewritten to work with 16 bits.

Is that such a big deal? What's the difference between an 8-bit processor and a 16-bit processor? To answer that, let's start by asking if you remember the Y2K computer disaster that did not happen? Almost all computers in 1999 used 8 bits to store the date in the form "99." Computer geeks were afraid that, on the stroke of midnight, the computers would store the date 2000 as "00" and interpret that to mean 1900. A single bit can represent 2 numbers, 0 and 1. Two bits can store four numbers, 0, 1, 2 and 3. Three bits can store eight numbers, 0 through 7. Let's jump ahead. Eight bits can store and represent $2^8 = 256$ numbers. So Eight bits can represent any two digit number and some three digit numbers, but it can not represent a number such as 1999. In the early days of computers, programmers were just getting off the ground. Writing programs (including machine code) for 8-bit numbers and strings was enough of a challenge. And at the time, 8 bits seemed like enough. Most displays were black and white. Color displays that used 8 bits (256 colors) looked fine. But it was natural to move to a 16-bit processor. Figure that $2^{16} = 65,563$, and you can do a lot more with 16 bits than with 8. But writing an operating system for 16 bits was more work than simply taking an 8-bit operating system and adding some new features. By the way, the majority of today's processors (2017) are 64-bit.

After being turned down by Digital Research, IBM went back

to Microsoft for advice. Gates and Allen had a reluctance to enter the OS market, but Microsoft gradually became involved. Paul Allen knew of a local company, Seattle Computer Products (SCP), that had written an OS for a 16-bit CPU. It was written by Tim Paterson and named the Quick and Dirty Operating System (QDOS). Digital Research had written an extensive operating manual for their CP/M operating system, and they provided it with every copy of CP/M that they licensed. Paterson was smart enough to read the manual and write the code for an OS that would function the same way, but would function using a 16 bit processor like the 8086. At that time, software was protected by Copyright law, which is weaker than Patent law. Later litigation by Digital Research claimed that Paterson copied their code, but their litigation was unsuccessful.

Allen called Seattle Computer Products and they arranged a license of QDOS to Microsoft for $10,000 plus $15,000 for every company that bought a subsequent license from Microsoft. In the continuing discussions with IBM, the IBM team showed no interest in writing an operating system. Neither were they interested in buying an operating system from Seattle Computer Products and maintaining it. Allen and Gates went back to Seattle Computer Products and bought QDOS outright for a total of $50,000. It's worth noting that business negotiations have no rules for symmetric transparency. IBM knew about Seattle Computer Products and QDOS, but Seattle Computer Products didn't know anything about the personal computer project at IBM and IBM's negotiations with Microsoft. Since you know all about diodes, we can make the analogy that Microsoft handled their negotiations like a diode; there was a one-way flow of information and that was a disadvantage for SCP.

Microsoft loaded QDOS onto floppy disks that were provided with the personal computer at the point of sale, and it was renamed PC-DOS (personal computer disk operating system). It became the grandfather of generations of desktop computer operating system software. One could argue that operating system software became a business activity worth tens or hundreds of billions of dollars and the purchase price of $50,000 for QDOS was one of the great bargains in history. Seattle Computer Products later took a complaint to court and the purchase price was raised to $1M. That's still one of the great bargains in history. IBM and Microsoft closed their deal in the fall of 1980. One feature in the agreement became of crucial importance and reveals the sharp business acumen of Bill Gates. Microsoft agreed to sell a license for PC-DOS to everyone who bought a PC, and to do so (initially) at the low cost of $40. However, they retained the right to sell a license for this operating system, which also became known as MS-DOS, to everyone who bought a personal computer similar to the IBM PC. In other words, they retained the right to license their operating system software to PC clones (note that clones wouldn't exist for another few years).

So let's review the key developments: IBM chose to use an open hardware architecture, which facilitated the cloning of their micro-computer. They also decided to outsource the OS. Microsoft bought the OS that was needed at a ridiculously low price. They decided on a closed software architecture. They owned the OS and retained the right to develop and modify it, and to license it to anyone who bought an IBM personal computer or a clone. IBM: open hardware architecture. Microsoft: closed software architecture. Which do you think proved to be the better strategy?

Let's take a broader view of the impact of Microsoft. The brilliant contribution of Bill Gates was to take two key principles from Ma Bell and apply them to software. First, like the phone company he developed a monopoly for OS software. He extended that monopoly to the broader software market. As of 2014, about 92% of personal computers used the Windows operating system. At the present time, the monopoly remains very strong (about 90%, 2017). Moving forward, the only thing that might weaken this monopoly is the trend towards mobile computing systems, for example smart phones and tablets, where other operating systems (like Android and Apple iOS) have a very large presence. Second, Gates adopted the idea that the consumer should not own anything. You, the individual, own your computer. But Microsoft created and owned a software product that was protected by copyright and patent law. You do not buy that product – you buy a license to use it. That software, a series of computer instructions, is fed into your computer and allows your computer to respond to your requests and to perform tasks. But you do not own the instructions that your computer uses. You own a license to use those instructions. That's not a subtle difference. If you owned the instructions, you would have the right to make a copy of them. You could give that copy to someone else or give that copy to another computer you own. That happened all the time in the early days of computing. Software was written by hobbyists. If they succeeded in writing a good program, they shared it with their friends. But the license business model places a stiff restriction on the dissemination of software – and thereby guarantees price control by the owner of the software. The owner might be the author, or it might be a person or company (Bill Gates) who hired the author. As computing devices have multiplied and spread and the cost per device has shrunk dramatically, software has shared the same multiplicative spread – but the cost per license has not shrunk dramatically. By some measures it actually increased. The first license for PC-DOS (1981) sold for $40. In 2016, a single Windows 10 license costs $120 ($200 for Windows 10 Pro).[4] According to the Bureau of Labor statistics, the inflated value of $40 in 1981 would be $106 in 2016. So the cost of a license has increased slightly. Of course, the Windows OS of 2016 does much more than the DOS of 1981. So the better comparison is with relative costs of personal computer hardware.

In 1993, Dell was selling a top-of-the-line 486 desktop with a 66MHz processor, eight megabytes of RAM and a 320-megabyte hard drive for $4,400.[5] In 2016, a high end Dell Inspiron 24 5000 series with Intel Core i5, 12 GB memory and 1TB hard drive sold for $900. That price includes the Windows 10 license ($125), so the price of the computer itself is about $775. The 2016 version has more internal memory by a factor of 1,500, and has more storage by a factor of 3,000. The speed is higher by a factor of 100. Comparing prices between 1993 and the present (2016), with no adjustment for inflation, the desktop price now is about 18% of the 1993 price. The comparison for software is quite different. The OS price now is 96% of the 1993 price. There is another way of stating this comparison. In 1981 the cost of the software (OS) of the first IBM PC was 2.5% of the cost of the complete system ($40 for software, $1,565 for the PC). In 1993 the cost of the software (OS) was 2.8% of the total price of the desktop. In 2016, the cost of the software was 14% of the total price. Software is king, and Bill Gates deserves much of the credit (if that's the right word) for the coronation. He is a brilliant businessman who honed the practices of the industrial barons of the 19th and 20th centuries and applied them to the high tech economy of the 21st century.

As software rose to dominance, beginning in the early 1990s, the door to financial success was opened to many other software entrepreneurs, especially for software used for internet applications. Mark Z and Facebook represent only one of the examples of neuveau software empires.[6] There was software for file sharing, for streaming, and for social media applications that spun off from Facebook. We'll look at these businesses shortly.

First, let's make a quantitative comparison of the business successes of IBM and Microsoft. Recall that around 1980 the largest computer company in the world decided to enter the micro-computer (aka personal computer) market and IBM CEO John Opel decided to choose an open architecture design. He also decided to outsource the software (the operating system) to an upstart company, Microsoft. Upstart CEO Bill Gates did not write open source (open architecture) OS software. He bought an appropriate OS from another company and packaged the OS for licensing to IBM PCs and also to any clone PC that used similar hardware. How did these business decisions work out for tech giant IBM and upstart Microsft?

We compare a measure of success of IBM and Microsoft by comparing the market capitalizations of the two companies over a period of three decades, as shown in Figure 5(a). In 1982, the market value of IBM was larger than that of Microsoft by a factor of approximately infinity. Microsoft's market capitalization (gray diamonds) is so small that it can't be distinguished from zero. IBM's market capitalization (open squares) was around $85B. It then plunged in the late 1980s and early 1990s. A portion of this drop may be related to their loss of share of PC market. IBM stayed in the PC business, running third behind HP and Dell, until 2005 when they sold that part of their business to Lenova.

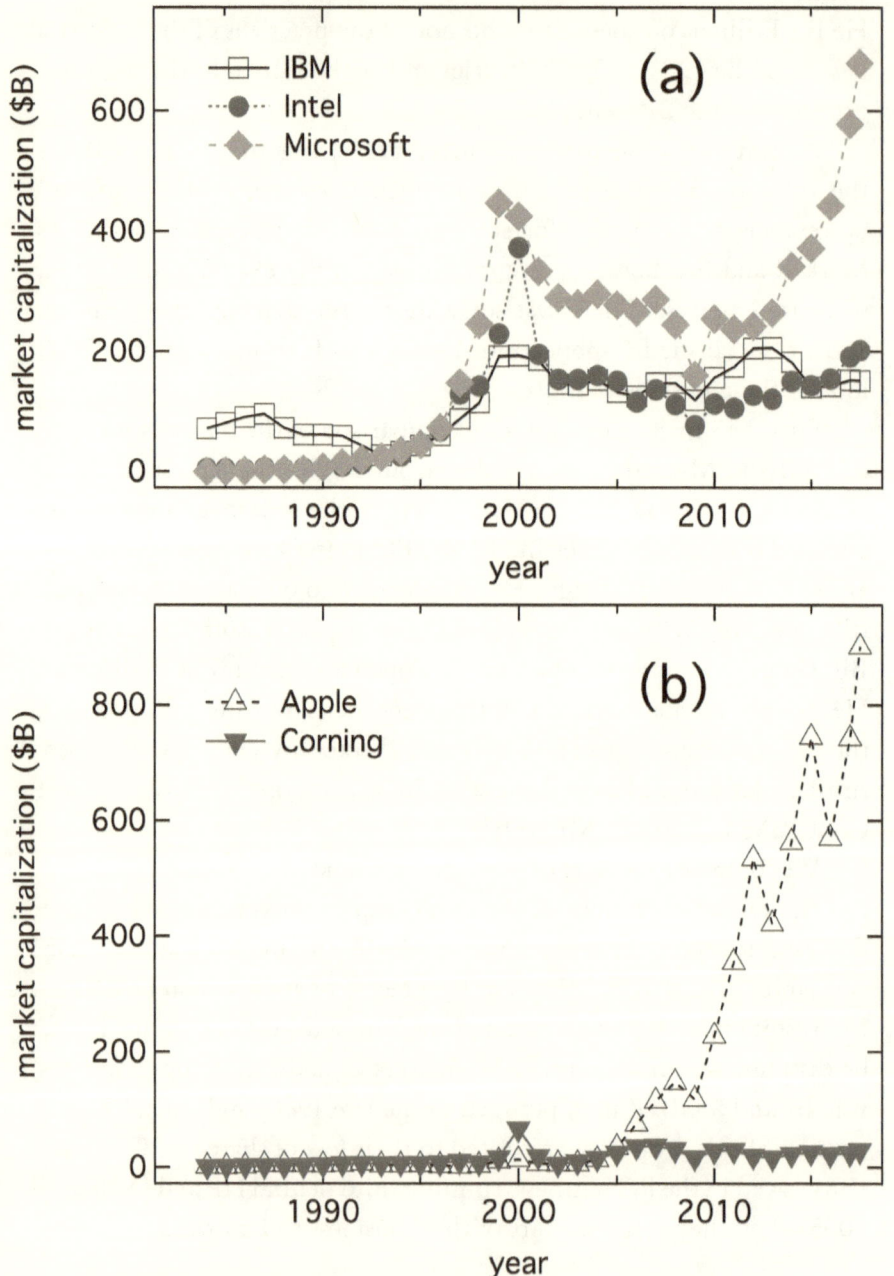

Figure 5(a, b). Market capitalizations of high tech companies since 1983: (a) IBM, Intel, and Microsoft and (b) Apple and Corning.

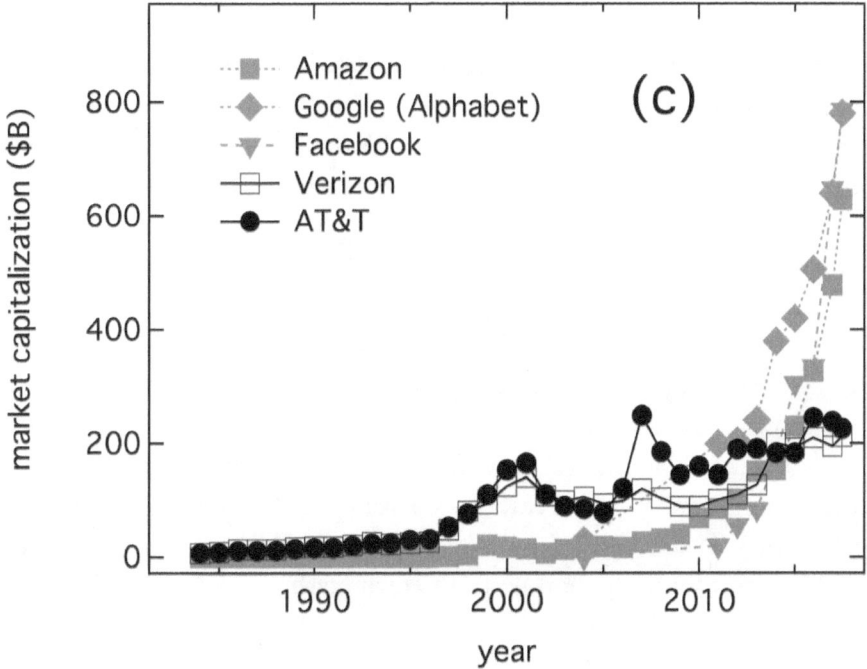

Figure 5(c). Market capitalizations of high tech (internet, social media, telecommunications) companies: Amazon, Alphabet, Facebook, Verizon and AT&T. For the data in all three panels, each data point is an approximate average of the market capitalization for the given year. For each company, the most recent datum is a single value from the first week of January, 2018, and is provided to help indicate current trends. Data were derived from several sources including ycharts.com and macrotrends.net.

The market cap of Microsoft is on a continual rise in this period and matches that of IBM in the mid 1990s. That's pretty remarkable. IBM was then a huge company with many tens of thousands of employees. IBM owned and operated many facilities including research laboratories. They had contributed to the development of the FET, and they had brought to market the first PC, a product that had a breakthrough effect on the microcomputer market. Microsoft was a small company with few physical assets and a relatively small number of employees. But it only took a few years for Microsoft to overtake IBM as measured by market cap.

Both IBM and Microsoft had increasing value in the late 90s. This was the tech boom or, more appropriately stated, the tech bubble. The bubble burst around 2000. Both companies showed a decreased market capitalization for a few years, but Microsoft had roughly twice the market cap. More broadly speaking, IBM enters the latter part of the 2010 decade with a market cap that's roughly double its value back in the early 1980s. Microsoft enters this time period with a market cap that's roughly triple that of IBM. One can say that Microsoft has benefited much more than IBM, an observation that's more glaring in the data trends of the past few years.

IBM is not unique. How has Intel fared? Intel co-invented the chip. Intel invented the 8086 microprocessor chip (released in 1978) that was used in the first IBM PC and the first generation of clones. The solid black circles in Figure 5(a) show the market capitalization of Intel over the same period of time. Intel was a very small company, compared with IBM, in the 1980s. Its market cap rose at a rate similar with that of Microsoft for the period up to the tech crash. After the tech bubble burst, Intel's market cap fell back to the same level as that of IBM and they have tracked together since then. Entering the latter part of the 2010 decade, Microsoft had a market cap about three times larger than that of Intel. Looking at Figure 5(a), one might conclude that hardware R&D was of little benefit to IBM and Intel, but was of tremendous benefit to Microsoft.

As a point of interest, the market capitalization of Apple is shown in Figure 5(b) using open triangles. Apple's market capitalization in the past few years has exceeded that of Microsoft and the left axis of panel (b) is extended to accommodate the larger value. Apple is an eclectic company, something of a hybrid mixture of hardware and software. The market share of Apple's personal computers has always hovered around 5% to 7% (though the profit margin for Apple computers is relatively high). The remarkable business success has come from innovations in consumer electronics that are associated with the vision of Steve Jobs, starting with the introduction of the iPod and iTunes in 2001 and continuing with the iPhone, introduced in 2007. Apple's market capitalization (approximately January 1, 2018), roughly $900B, is the largest of any publicly traded company in the US.

A similar comparison can be made for the companies centrally involved in the fiber optic telecommunications network. The primary hardware company is Corning. Briefly, Corning was one of the top ten largest tech companies, as measured by market cap. Another hardware company is Verizon. The courts split AT&T into eight separate companies in an anti-monopoly action in 1984. AT&T kept its name and the long-distance calling business. The rest of the company was split into seven "regional Bell operating companies." Two of these companies, Bell South and NYNEX, became Verizon. Verizon built and now operates a fiber optic network and also operates a cellular phone network and service. Examples of software companies that use this network are Google and Facebook. Neither of these offers a physical product. Both offer a web-based service that is based on the physical telecommunications networks. Amazon is a company that is a web-based software service, but Amazon provides physical products as part of that service.

Figure 5(b) shows the market capitalization of Corning with solid black triangles. Corning was traditionally a small company with an unusually large commitment to research. Their market cap shows a peak during the tech bubble circa 2000. Since then it has continued to be a small company (market cap of about $25B). The market caps of Google and Facebook are shown with filled gray symbols, diamonds and triangles, respectively, in Figure 5(c). These two companies show a meteoric rise since their inception. The market cap of Amazon is shown with filled gray squares. Amazon has the longest history of the three and its sharp rise began in the last few years of the 2000 decade. It can be mentioned that the two companies with the fastest growth (Google and Facebook) are purely software companies. Each has a minimal physical footprint and few physical assets. The open gray squares show the market cap of Verizon. Transoceanic fiber optic cables were in service in the mid 1990s. Verizon started laying fiber optic cable in the late 1990s and some terrestrial networks were in service by 2000. Verizon's market cap saw growth during this era, as they have profited from the ability to charge customers for using the network that the customers paid to have installed. As mentioned above, a federal court antitrust ruling broke up the old AT&T in early 1984. Crudely speaking, the present companies Verizon and AT&T together equal the old Bell phone company. The market capitalization of AT&T is shown with black circles in Figure 5(c). It's success has tracked very closely with that of Verizon. These two companies have a better business model than that of Corning. Corning invented the fiber optic cable, then made and sold it, and that was it – they went back to where they were before. As Verizon enters the latter part of the 2010 decade, their value is growing from increased use of the mobile platform, and their market cap is larger than either IBM or Intel.

The market capitalization charts show that the software industry is explosively profitable. From the game we played in Chapter 2, we learned that many of the most affluent people in the world came to their fortune in this industry. These fortunes are so spectacular that I propose we invent a new unit of wealth. I call it the *Zuckr*, and one Zuckr = $50 B. This is the fortune that Mark Z acquired by age 30. It didn't take a lifetime to build. It took about 10 years and he wasn't hard at work for all that time. This is a convenient unit when one talks about large sums of money. The market capitalization of IBM is about 3 Zuckrs. The same for Intel. The market cap of Facebook is about 7 Zuckrs.

Looking back at the answer sheet for Table 1, the people associated with software have personal wealth on the order of 0.1 to 1 Zuckr. But people associated with hardware inventions have smaller personal wealth, on the order of 0.0001 Zuckr. We can invent two more new units, the mini-Zuckr and the micro-Zuckr. The personal wealth of the best of the hardware inventors is on the order of a tenth of a milli-Zuckr, if not less. The notable exception in Table 1 is Robert Noyce, co-founder of Intel. J. Jim Hsieh also did well in the private sector of diode laser production. In the US, the median net worth of a household with a head of household who is about 50 years old (prime working years) is about 1 micro-Zuckr. If you identify with this demographic, then Mark Z is worth more than you by a factor of 1 million.

Some reasons for the disparity in wealth between hardware and software entrepreneurs can be identified. The first reason is that the hardware inventors came first. They invented and developed the pieces of a physical and technical platform and the value of the platform was not yet known. The software entrepreneurs who saw the potential for the platform deserve credit for creating value. On the other hand, just about anyone should be able to predict that a communications cable with 1 million times more bandwidth than the best existing cable is going to be valuable. A transistor that uses a millionth of the power of the best existing transistor also is going to be pretty valuable.

A second reason involves a bigger picture. There is a logical thread in patent law that goes like this: an invention is owned by the tools (machines) that make it. A similar thread is found in experimental research: data are owned by the apparatus (machine) that acquires the data. Of course a machine does not have ownership rights, so the rights belong to the person or company or agency that owns the machine. This is an extension of a basic principle of capitalism. Equipment is a form of capital, a capital investment. The things made by the equipment should pay a return on that capital investment. When a researcher accepts employment from a company, university or government agency, he/she agrees to terms that typically include a statement that an idea that is not related to his/her work responsibilities may belong to the researcher. However, if the researcher uses any tools of the company or agency then that company or agency owns the IP.

That's an obstacle for hardware research. The Wright brothers built their airplane in their own shop. They owned the tools. They were granted a patent (US patent no. 821,393; May, 1906) for their airplane and owned all the rights to the patent. They had all the legal weight that they needed to turn their work into a business success, but still they had trouble making money from their invention. Initially there was almost no market for airplanes. After the market improved, they had long patent fights with many other companies that were entering the aviation business. Wilbur died and Orville sold the Wright Company, in 1915, for $250,000 ($6.1M in 2017 dollars). That's not very much for the immense contribution they made. They created the aeronautics industry.

Thomas Edison built his first invention, in 1869 at age 22, in his garage. It was an improved stock ticker (The Universal Stock Printer). He owned all the rights and sold the patent to The Gold and Stock Telegraph Company for $40,000 (about $1.1M in 2017 dollars). He used that money to set up a small lab in Newark. He owned his own tools and hired a few machinists, so he owned all the rights to all his inventions. He then followed the natural course of business. He hired entrepreneurs who worked in his lab. He owned the tools. If they discovered something, then Edison's company owned the patent. At his death in October of 1931, Edison's wealth was about $12M ($195M in 2017 dollars), equivalently about 8 milli-Zuckr.[7]

In the present times, someone interested in high tech hardware may wish to invent something. He/she can go to work for a company, university or agency, but they own the machines and they own the IP. They might return a small payment to the inventor. Or not. There is no such obstacle for software. The tool needed to invent/create software is a computer. Everyone owns a computer - or two or three or more. You can invent new code on your own laptop. You own the tools. You own the IP.

If you try a software venture there is little risk and little cost. A venture capitalist might stake you and a few co-workers to a year or two of salary and rent for a small space. There are many such ventures. If one fails, the people involved have little trouble moving on to another venture - or to a more traditional software job. By contrast, a hardware venture has high cost and more risk. The startup cost includes the cost of equipment, money and time to install and assemble the equipment, plus maintenance and repair for the equipment. If the venture fails, the equipment is a large expense that's lost. In hardware research, if you are part of a failed venture then that's an obstacle to overcome if you try to move on to a new venture.

Here is a review of some characteristics of hardware and software research:

Hardware	Software
Research and development:	
Requires laboratory facilities	Requires a laptop
Expensive, corporate investment $0.1B to $10B	Affordable to any individual $1K to 1$M
R&D takes many years	R&D is fast, 1 month to 1 year

Intellectual property

IP is owned by the owner of R&D facilities; may share a small portion with inventor	IP is owned by the inventor

From the perspectives of business as well as personal psychology and motivation, it's easy to see why software has become the dominant area of high tech research and development.

CHAPTER

11

How Big Are Software Empires?

There have been occasions when the government has recognized an extraordinary need for the pursuit of a scientific goal and has stepped in to pursue and achieve the goal. General skepticism about the efficacy of government wisdom and the effectiveness of its bureaucracy is well founded. However, there have been several famous cases where the government stepped up and the result was dramatic, unparalleled success. These cases involved massive resources and huge expense. One example is the Manhattan Project.

Many historians agree that three technological achievements were crucially significant in the victory of the Allied forces. (1) Several developments involving radar. The basic principles of radar were known in the 1880s, following laboratory experiments with radio wave reflection by Heinrich Hertz. The first practical radar system was built by the British, in 1935, under the design and direction of physicist Sir Robert Watson-Watt, and used long wavelengths ($f = 25$ MHz; wavelength $\lambda = 10$ m). Developments in the US and elsewhere led to better systems and shorter wavelengths ($f = 200$ MHz; $\lambda \sim 1$ m). But the real breakthrough came when British engineers Harry Boot and John Randall invented the *cavity magnetron* in early 1940, a small, compact and powerful generator of microwaves. Magnetrons were small enough to fit in airplanes and submarine conning towers, but they could generate microwaves (λ = 10 cm) with a power of 400 W. This was enough power for a useful radar beam. (2) Code breaking. The Americans broke the Japanese code early in the war, and the work of Alan Turing and his British group at Bletchley Park broke the code of the Nazi Enigma machine. The Turing story is told very well by Andrew Hodges.[1] (3) The development of the atomic bomb.

The atomic bomb was not solely responsible for ending the war with Japan, but all historians would agree that the end was reached sooner because of it. The Manhattan project was a tremendously successful government research and development project, with the specific goal of building an atomic bomb. The project had several separate components. The largest part (largest when categorized by expense and number of personnel; 63% of all budget expenditures) was at Oak Ridge, TN, where the fissile material (Uranium) was derived from ore and purified. Two separate approaches were used. *Calutrons* were large electromagnetic *mass spectrometers*. Individual atoms would be given an electric charge (ionized) and then injected into a vacuum chamber in a large magnetic field. The atom would move in a curved trajectory with a radius that depended on its mass. The trajectories of U_{235} and U_{238} atoms are slightly different. The U_{235} atoms were captured. In this way, the pure U_{235} material for the bomb was built up one atom at a time. The Calutrons were huge electromagnets and required a huge amount of electricity. While they were operating, usually at night, they used 14% of all the electricity produced in the US. This process wasn't very efficient so the Oak Ridge Lab also had a plan B. They built a large facility for isotope separation by *gaseous diffusion*. Ultimately, this produced most of the Uranium for the bombs.

Plan C, in case there wasn't enough Uranium, was to use Plutonium. Three nuclear reactors were built at Hanford, WA. This was a gutsy thing to do. These were production scale reactors, designed and built after a single working predecessor reactor was built – that being Fermi's test reactor at the Univ. of Chicago. The Hanford reactors (21% of all budget expenditures) were for the production of Plutonium. By the end of the war, the Manhattan project had made and delivered three bombs: one Uranium (*Little Boy*, used at Hiroshima) and two plutonium (*Gadget*, used for the Trinity test; and *Fat Man*, used at Nagasaki). The portion of the Manhattan project that took place at Los Alamos, NM, is perhaps the most famous part. It's been the subject of several books and movies. It involved the research, design, development and assembly of the bombs and represented about 4% of the budget.

The Project lasted about two years, gearing up by the summer of 1943 and phasing out after the summer of 1945. It employed about 125,000 people at the peak. Among those employed were several who became Nobel laureates in physics: Hans Bethe, Richard Feynman, Leo Szilard, Enrico Fermi, Ernest Lawrence, Emilio Segre and Glen Seaborg. There were others who are equally famous but did not win a Nobel prize: examples are Robert Oppenheimer, Edward Teller and Robert Wilson.

All historians agree that the Manhattan project was instrumental in bringing the war to its end. Of course, it did more. For better or worse, nuclear weapons became a revolutionary new class of weapons. They dominated the Cold War. They will dominate strategic war planning for the foreseeable future. The Hanford nuclear reactors were the first demonstration of a production nuclear energy facility. They represent the key technological development, and significant intellectual property, for what became the nuclear power industry. Whether you like nuclear power or don't like it, there are about 450 nuclear power plants in the world. Each is an investment of around $2B, so the industry has a capitalization of roughly $1T.

And what was the final cost of this tremendously significant project? Actually, it was pretty cheap. The entire cost was about ½ Zuckr ($25B in 2017 dollars). In other words, if the Manhattan Project was needed today, Mark Z could pay for the entire thing by writing a check. And he'd still have half his wealth left over.

A second example is best known metaphorically as an undertaking that has very high risks (a goal for success that's nearly impossible to reach), but – if successful - has unique and unprecedented rewards. This would be the original "moon shot," the Apollo Program. In the spring of 1961, President J. F. Kennedy addressed a joint session of Congress and proclaimed a new goal for the United States, to "commit itself to achieving the goal, before this decade is out, of landing a man on the Moon and returning him safely to the Earth." He further explained this goal in a speech at Rice University, September 1962:[2] "Surely the opening vistas of space promise high costs and hardships, as well as high reward…. [the] hazards are hostile to us all. Its conquest deserves the best of all mankind, and its opportunity for peaceful cooperation may never come again. But why, some say, the moon? Why choose this as our goal? And they may well ask why climb the highest mountain? Why, 35 years ago, fly the Atlantic? Why does Rice play Texas? … We choose to go to the moon in this decade and do the other things, not because they are easy, but because they are hard, because that goal will serve to organize and measure the best of our energies and skills, because that challenge is one that we are willing to accept, one we are unwilling to postpone, and one which we intend to win…." Set in a time of fervor surrounding the "space race," the Apollo program received remarkably bipartisan support in Congress and around the country. The Apollo program started in 1959 and ramped up quickly in 1961, reaching peak funding in 1963. It ended in 1974. At the peak, the program employed about 400,000 people, 34,000 NASA employees and 375,000 government contractors. The majority of the funds were spent on designing, building testing and perfecting the systems and rockets needed to get men to the moon and then safely home again.[3]

Much of the infrastructure already existed. Missiles and rockets had been developed starting in the 1940s. Robert Goddard was a key US figure. Nazi Germany developed the V1 and V2 rockets. Werner von Braun and several of his associates came to the US after the war. By the late 1950s, rocket engines were in production. A much larger rocket would be needed to serve as the launch vehicle. The vehicle that would take the astronauts to the moon and back had two parts, the command / service module (CSM) and the lunar module (LM). On the launch pad, the total height of the rocket (Apollo spacecraft plus Saturn V rocket) was taller than the length of a football field, about 130 yards.

The Saturn V rocket had 3 stages. The first stage had five rocket engines that were fueled by liquid oxygen and kerosene. The five engines produced about 7 ½ million pounds of thrust. This number may be hard to grasp. The engines pushed the rocket to an altitude of about 36 miles and reached a speed of 1.7 miles per second. If the Saturn V had malfunctioned and exploded at liftoff, the explosion would have been equivalent to ½ kilotons of TNT. Compare this with the explosive force of the bomb that destroyed the entire city of Hiroshima, 13 kilotons. It's 4% of that force, and it was devoted to only 3 people. The astronauts were sitting on top of a very large bomb which was detonated in a controlled fashion. When stage 1 had burned all its fuel, exploding bolts separated the burned out stage from the rest of the vehicle. The second stage also had 5 engines and produced a thrust of about 1.1 million pounds. This stage took the vehicle to an altitude of about 100 miles. Stage 3 had a single engine that produced about 0.2 million pounds of thrust. This stage was used to reach earth orbit, with a height of about 140 miles, and a velocity approximately equal to earth's escape velocity, about 7 miles per second (Mach 33). When the trajectory was appropriate for starting the path to the moon, the stage 3 rocket was used again.

History records that the Apollo 11 mission was the first time a human walked on the surface of the moon, touching the surface on July 20, 1969. Most people forget all the practice runs. There were many unmanned launches to test the Saturn V rocket. There were numerous tests of the CSM, including the tragic and fatal test, January 1967, that ended with a fire that took the lives of astronauts Gus Grissom, Ed White and Roger Chaffee. This tragedy shut down further testing for a year and a half. The first manned flight test was the Apollo 7 mission, with liftoff on Oct. 11, 1968. Three astronauts orbited earth for 11 days testing equipment. Then there were 3 "practice" trips to the moon. Apollo 8 and 9 went to the moon, entered lunar orbit and then returned to earth. Apollo 10 went to the moon, and then two astronauts tested the lunar module. While the CSM was in lunar orbit at a height of about 70 miles, the lunar module separated from the CSM. It performed several lunar orbits on its own, descending to a lunar height of about 9 miles, a bit higher than the flight path of a commercial jet airplane over earth. It regained height, docked with the CSM, and then the mission returned to earth.

Apollo 11, launched July 16, 1969, was a truly dramatic event and represents a milestone in the history of mankind. Historians and journalists have written about it extensively and I cannot add more.

Apollo 12 was launched in November, 1969, during a lull in a thunderstorm. The rocket was struck by lightening about 30 second after liftoff. Portions of the electrical system were destroyed. The command module went dark. The commander, Pete Conrad, was ready to push the "abort" button but didn't. He decided to wait. The rocket was struck by a second bolt of lightening about 15 seconds later. So much for the old saying that lightening never strikes the same place twice. These were the days of the "Right Stuff.[4]" A young flight controller (a 24 year old engineer) at Mission Control remembered the protocol for rebooting the flight computer. In spite of all the confusion, he managed to get his message to the crew and Alan Bean, recognizing what to do, was able to reboot the computer.[5] A few days later, Conrad and Bean became the second two man crew to walk on the moon. They landed about 800 feet from their intended site. Pretty good for a 240,000 mile trip and a computer with less computing power than a smart watch. Conrad and Bean collected geologic samples and set up scientific instruments, including a seismograph.

Apollo 13 was famously unlucky. Apollo 15, 16 and 17 were successful and relatively uneventful. Astronauts were driving vehicles and swing golf clubs on the moon. It seemed like the drama was receding and the public was losing interest. Still, every moon shot was a staggering technological achievement.

And what was the final cost of this tremendously significant project? More than the Manhattan Project, but still pretty cheap: about 2.6 Zuckrs. The cumulative cost of Program Apollo was about $20.4B. A more accurate figure accounts for inflation during the course of the project. When calculated using 1975 dollars, the total cost was $29.3B.[6] Inflation from 1975 to early 2017 is a factor of 4.49, which means the cost in 2017 dollars is $132B. That's about 2.6 Zuckrs. If we chose to undertake the Apollo project again, Mark Z. would be unable to write the check. However, if a few of today's billionaires would each write a check for half their fortune then the total would be more than enough.

It seems like the Zuckr is a large amount of money. It begs the question, how does the wealth of Mark Z and other software magnates compare with that of famously wealthy people in our past? In the industrial era from roughly 1800 through the mid 1950s, a number of famous entrepreneurs achieved great fortunes. Examples of several industrial barons are given below and each achieved great wealth.

Other examples may be found in the field of finance and banking and I mention a single example. John Pierpoint Morgan was the son of a banker. He inherited some wealth from his father. Of greater importance he inherited a number of banking connections. His father arranged an alliance between J. P. and Anthony Drexel in 1871 and the Drexel Morgan investment bank was born. Drexel Morgan made lucrative investments in railroads and reportedly bailed out both GE and the US government during the depression of 1893. Drexel Morgan later bought US Steel from Andrew Carnegie. J. P. Morgan became famous as figure of wealth, but we will see that his net worth, about $45B (2017 dollars) and a little less than 1 Zuckr, is rather paltry compared with the wealth accumulated by the industrial giants.

Cornelius Vanderbilt is famous for living a true rags-to-riches story. He started work at age 11 (1805) by working on his father's boat. His fortune began with a loan of a thousand dollars (about $25,000 in 2017 dollars), which he used to start a ferry service across New York harbor. He expanded his business to include steamships and then had greater success with railroads. By the time of his death in 1877, his fortune was estimated at $167B to $185B (2017 dollars), about 3.5 Zuckrs.[7]

Henry Ford was born into a farming family in Michigan. He started work in Detroit at age 16 as an apprentice machinist. For the next ten years he worked on his family farm, did factory work, and operated a sawmill. At 28 he got a job as engineer, working for the Edison Lighting Company in Detroit, rising to the position of chief engineer in two years. He tinkered with automobiles, finishing his first car (the quadricycle) in 1896. He sold the quadricycle to raise funds. He attracted some funding from investors and quit his job at Edison Lighting. A first automobile company was started in 1899. Ford left the company in 1902 after disagreements with investors. That company later became the Cadillac Motor Car Company. In 1903 he started the Ford Motor Company. The Model T was introduced in 1908 and was an immediate success. Ford's ideas for mass production were in place within a few years. By 1918 half of all the cars in America were Model T Fords. A battle with shareholders in 1920 was led by Horace and John Dodge. In response, Ford bought out the minority stock holders. His later years were marred by his controversial anti-Semitic opinions. The peak of his personal fortune, in 1917 at age 57 (thirty years before his death), is estimated to be $188B to $198B (2017 dollars), about 3 ¾ Zuckrs.[8] As an aside, former employer Thomas Edison didn't fare so well. While many consider Edison to be America's most successful inventor, his peak wealth was about $0.2B (2017 dollars), about 0.008 Zuckrs.

Andrew Carnegie was born in Scotland. His father worked as a weaver and both parents were active supporters of worker's rights. As power looms began to dominate the textile industry, Andrew's family decided to emigrate to America and settled in a town near Pittsburgh. At age 13, Andrew started work as a bobbin boy in a cotton factory. At 14 he became a telegraph messenger. By 18 he was the private secretary and personal messenger of the superintendent of the Pennsylvania Railroad Company. Six years later he became the superintendent of the Pittsburgh division of the company. With this position, he began making clever investments in railroads, oil fields and steel mills.

The bulk of his fortune was made with the steel industry. He founded the Carnegie Steel Company, which had domineering success. He then sold it to JP Morgan as the US Steel Company. Estimates of his personal fortune vary. In one estimate it reached a peak of about $300B (2017 dollars), 6 Zuckrs, in 1903 when Carnegie was 68. Carnegie was probably a ruthless businessman and the bloody Homestead strike is famous in the history of bad labor relations. However, Carnegie is also famous as a philanthropist. He gave away 90% of his fortune to charity before his death. By some estimates, Carnegie was the wealthiest American who ever lived.[9]

But there are other estimates that suggest that the largest fortune produced by anyone born in the US belonged to John D. Rockefeller. His father was a travelling salesman, of sorts, selling "cures" (or at least treatments) for diseases including cancer. The father was away for long periods of time but provided the family with a good income. When the family moved to Owego, NY, John studied at a private academy and excelled in math. He started working, in 1855 (age 16), as a bookkeeper in Cleveland. He started his first business at age 19, in partnership with a neighbor, as a wholesale merchant of grain, meat, and other merchandise. Their first year, 1859, was very successful. The Civil War began the next year and business boomed. His fortune took off when he entered a new business. A patent for distilling kerosene from oil had been granted in 1850 to chemist James Young. Oil was discovered in Pennsylvania in 1859, kicking off an oil boom. Rockefeller bought into an oil refining company in 1863. Two years later (at age 24), he bought out his partners and began expanding the business. In 1866 he brought his brother into the business and they built a large refinery in Cleveland, which they named the Standard Works. The Rockefellers added another partner, Henry Flagler, and by 1867 the firm was the largest oil refiner in the world. Standard Oil of Ohio was formed in January of 1870. John (age 31) was the majority shareholder with 30% ownership. His brother had 14%. By all accounts John was a ruthless businessman who created a nearly perfect monopoly. Standard Oil had 90% of market share for refined oil. In the early days of the company, refined oil was kerosene that was used for light and heat. At the time of his death in 1937 his wealth was estimated to be about $350B (2017 dollars), 7 Zuckrs. This amount represented about 1.5% of the US economic output.[10]

There are some commonalities in these stories. For one, by today's standards all these entrepreneurs started out as child laborers. They began working at ages ranging from 11 to 16. Today, a sixteen-year old worker would be considered a child laborer. Although John Rockefeller started with a trade (bookkeeper), the others started out doing labor or some other kind of blue collar work. This contrasts with the stories of today's software magnates. Bill Gates, Mark Z, and most (if not all) of the others came from wealthy families. Not one is known to have worked jobs that involved physical labor (with an exception for Jeff Bezos, who had a summer job at a fast food restaurant).

The wealth of the software magnates of today, with fortunes of about 1 Zuckr, is comparable with the wealth of the titans of the industrial era. However, a couple of differences can be noted. First, Mark Z and other software magnates acquired their wealth fairly quickly, in about 10 years. In other words, the rate of wealth creation is high. Second, ships have been around for millennia. The locomotive was successfully demonstrated in 1804 in Scotland, but it was 25 years before work on the network of rail tracks began. That work went on for 3 decades and Cornelius Vanderbilt, one of the first to make part of his fortune from railroads, didn't get that part of his fortune until the late 1860s, some 60 years after the first locomotive. By contrast, software didn't exist at all until the late 1960s. By the late 1980s, software companies were making great wealth. By 1995, Bill Gates was listed as the wealthiest man in America, less than 30 years from the beginning of commercial software.

There is another commonality about the nature of the fortunes of these industrial magnates, one which offers a striking difference with the software industry fortunes derived in the 21st century. For the former, the fortunes were built on tangible assets. The businesses involved physical commodities. Tangible infrastructure was involved, such as factories, railroad tracks and highways. By contrast, software is a collection of bits. There is nothing tangible about bits. Software is a category of computer instructions. The instructions are presented to a machine (a computer) as a stream of bits. Bits are quite ethereal. Looking at the plots of market cap for different companies, until the recent past it was unprecedented to have a company with a large fortune based on bits. It seems to defy the laws of supply and demand. There is an endless supply of bits. How does the law of supply and demand work when there is no limit to the supply?[11]

The development of the high tech industry (including both hardware and software), with a history that includes exponential growth, near collapse, and exponential growth again, reflects its unusual status regarding standard economic forces. As discussed in earlier chapters, computers in the 1950s were large and expensive and were not widely used outside government and military laboratories. The industry came into existence, with real economic impact, in the 1960s. The IBM 360, which also was large but not as large as prior mainframes, was relatively inexpensive and ran software that readily could be mastered and shared across platforms. The desktop computer business started a decade later and rapidly gained traction. Tim Burners-Lee, a British physicist, was one of the inventors of the *internet* and *world wide web*.[12] The internet became available to the public in 1991. Commercially available browsers were released in the early 1990s. Microsoft released its browser (Internet Explorer 1) in 1995. The world wide web established computers as a hardware platform for an entirely new form of communication. It opened the possibility of an entirely new form of business enterprise. The high tech industry enjoyed exponential growth in the 1990s. This was followed by explosive growth that resulted in a classic investment bubble.

In 1980 the global market capitalization of high tech companies was about $50B, representing about 1.5% of all global equity valuations.[13] By 1990 the global market cap had increased by more than a factor of 3, to about $175B. In the 1990s the valuations rocketed upwards. At the zenith, in 2000, the global market cap reached $8T and represented about 25% of world equity valuations. That figure is hard to grasp. In the next three years the bottom fell out for high tech valuations, and the global market cap fell to about $3T. By 2012 the figure had come back to about $7T, approximately 15% of world equity valuations. The figure has continued to grow in the last five years.

Another trend also is noteworthy. In 1990 the ten largest high technology industries were IBM, Verizon, AT&T, HP, Motorola, Intel, Nortel, Microsoft, Apple and Corning. They represented 80% of the high tech valuations. Ten years later, in 2000, the top ten companies represented only 5% of valuations. Much of the other valuation was in Initial Private Offers (IPOs). Many of these failed, and a few years later the top ten companies held about 30% of high tech valuations. In 1990 the telecommunications companies and computer (hardware) manufacturers dominated the top ten companies. IBM alone had about 35% of the market capitalization of the top ten. In 2000, software surpassed hardware and became king of high tech. Information technology spending grew quickly as companies bought the latest software. Microsoft passed IBM, and Oracle was close behind. The telecomm companies were making money by deploying the network infrastructure to interconnect literally millions of terminals. The period that began around 2008 or so brought the boom in mobile technology. Apple rose to the top and Samsung grew rapidly. The mobile carriers, like AT&T, Verizon, China Mobile and Vodaphone also rose to the top ranks.

While I'm discussing these trends now in broad terms, I remarked on them earlier in Chapter 15. The tech bubble is easily identified in the plots of market capitalization in Figures 5(a) and (b). These plots clearly show the next interesting development. Within a few years, software companies such as Microsoft and Oracle were again experiencing exponential growth. New companies based on software, such as Facebook and Google, were born after the tech bubble and have experienced steady exponential growth. The picture is very different for hardware companies. IBM and Intel, the classic examples of high tech hardware, stabilized after the tech crash. However, their post-bubble growth has been slow and incremental. The market cap of IBM in 2015 is larger than the 1990 market cap by a factor of about 2.3. For Intel the ratio is about 22. Compare this with Microsoft, where the ratio is 63. Apple is a unique case because it has always been both a hardware and software company. Apple's market cap in 2016 was about 184 times higher than it was in 1990. Apple has always developed hardware products, including desktop and laptop computers. But it always developed its own software for these products: the Mac operating system, which has been the single largest (and it's not very large, by market share) competitor with Microsoft operating systems. Apple has had dramatic ups and downs, many related to the ups and downs and the strong personality of Steve Jobs. But it owes its explosive growth to the development of both new software and hardware. Most recently, its products have helped generate the high tech shift to mobile devices. Hardware examples are the iPod, iPad, and iPhone. Examples of the former are iTunes, the App Store and Apple TV. Most people would acknowledge that iTunes revolutionized the music industry.

So let me summarize what I believe to be quite unusual. By 2015, the high tech industry composed about 15% of the global economy (measured by market cap).[13] As we will see in a later chapter, the five largest high tech companies in the US make up 12% of the entire US market capitalization of publicly held companies. About 7% of the US GDP comes *directly from software* ($1T out of $14T, 2014).[14] The US civilian labor force is about 160 million. Software employs about 2.5 million people.[14] Thus, about 1.5% of the labor force contributes 7% of the GDP. The post-bubble recovery has been led by software. What's remarkable is that an industry that didn't exist 40 years ago has grown to be a dominant force in business. The rate of growth continues to be very high. Furthermore, a fairly large number people associated with the industry have acquired great wealth in a short time. It would seem that the software industry has low barriers for entry. One doesn't need to build, acquire or manipulate a physical infrastructure. The key commodity is bits. Bits are easy and inexpensive to make and to reproduce. Bits represent a new form of "capital."

Finally, the people who created the physical platform that software serves have missed out on capturing the largest portion of high tech wealth. The people who create the software that uses that platform completely dominate the accumulation of high tech wealth.

CHAPTER

12

A Brief History of Wealth in the US

High technology has risen to become a significant, if not dominant, part of our economy. Within high tech, software has turned the tables on hardware and now software is completely supreme. The software sector has accumulated a lot of success and wealth. Historically, Mark Z's wealth is not an aberration, as seen in the last chapter. The industrial barons of the nineteenth and early twentieth centuries had net worth values of several Zuckrs. Nevertheless, there are several things that are unusual about software wealth.

* * * * *

1) There have been very wealthy people at various times in US history. However, the wealth of Mark Z (and other software magnates) is quite high in the history of the last 40 years.

2) Software did not exist 40 years ago and became a sector of the economy only within the last 30 years. However, it has risen quickly and provides a substantial portion of the US and global economies, as measured by market capitalization.

3) The wealth generated by software is highly concentrated. Software billionaires dominate the list of the wealthiest people in the US to a degree unlike what has ever been seen before. I will consider the high technology industry to include hardware, software and internet businesses and will lump the internet components along with software. The high technology industry composed about 15% of the global economy (2012).[1] Using Bureau of Labor statistics classifications, it accounted for 12% of employment and 23% of output of the US economy (2014).[2] As noted in the last chapter, 7% of the US economic output is directly related to software alone. But 6 out of the 10 wealthiest Americans in 2016 derived their wealth from the software industry. This suggests that software wealth is highly concentrated.

*　*　*　*　*

Let's start with (1). Forbes began compiling lists of the world's most wealthy people in 1982.[3] By 1987 it was annual event. It's a bit daunting to identify the wealthiest people in the decades before 1982, without the helpful research of the Forbes staff. Still, some speculations can be made. Howard Hughes is often acknowledged as the wealthiest American from the mid 1960s until his death in 1976.[4] In the early 1980s, the wealthiest Americans included Gordon Getty, who inherited the oil wealth of his father, J. Paul Getty (about $4B in 1984); Sam Walton, founder of WalMart (about $2.8B in 1985); and Ross Perot, founder of Electronic Data Systems, a company specializing in high tech hardware, computers and data processing systems (about $1.8B in 1985).

For the last three decades, we can get an idea of how wealth has been generated, and how the wealth at the top was distributed, by looking at a few snapshots of the Forbes list. We start with 1990:

The 1990 Forbes 400 list: This is an international list. For the convenience of a following discussion, I separately number the Americans in their order of wealth using brackets. Figures in parentheses are adjusted for inflation to 2017 dollars (a factor of 1.85).

*　*　*　*　*　*　*　*

1) Sultan Haji Waddaulah, $25B ($46.2B), Oil and gas, Brunei
2) King Fahd Al Saud, $18B ($33.3B), Oil and gas, Saudi Arabia
3) [1] Forrest Mars Sr. and family, $12.5B ($23.1B), candy and food, US
4) Queen Elizabeth II, 11.7B ($21.6B), real estate and more, UK
5) [2] Samuel and Donald Newhouse, $11.5B ($21.3B), publications and broadcasting, New York, US
6) Albert, Paul and Ralph Reichmann, $11B ($20.3B), various (not high tech), Canada
7) Y. Tsutsumi, $7.5B ($13.9B), railways, Japan
8) [3] Sam Walton and family, WalMart, $7.3B ($13.5B), US
9) [4] John Kluge, $7B ($13.0B), real estate & investments, Virginia, US
10) Tsai Wan-Lin and Tsai Wan-Tsai, $6.5B ($12.0B), life insurance, construction, Taiwan
11) Kenneth Thomson, $6.2B ($9.6B), real estate, Canada
12) Kichinosuke Sasaki, $5.7B ($10.6B), real estate, Japan
13) Gerald Grosvenor, $5.4B ($10.0B), real estate, UK
14) Sheikh Jaber Al Sabah, 4.8B ($8.9B), investments, Kuwait
15) [5] Charles and David Koch, $4.7B ($8.7B), oil and other investments, New York, US
16) [6] Anne Chambers, $4.5B ($8.3B), Cox enterprise (media), Hawaii, US
17) [7] Perry Bass and family, $4.5B ($8.3B), oil, real estate, investments, Texas, US
18) [8] Jay and Robert Pritzker, $4.5B ($8.3B), Hyatt (hotel and resorts), Chicago, US
19) Queen Beatrix, $4.8B ($8.9B), securities, real estate, jewels, Netherlands
20) Thomas Schmidheiny and family, $4.2B ($7.8B), construction, investments, Netherlands
21) Giovanni Agnelli, $4.0B ($7.4B), real estate, Italy
22) Sheikh Rashid Al Maktoum and family, $4.0B ($7.4B), oil, U. Arab Emirates
23) Johanna Quandt and family, $4.0B ($7.4B), securities, BMW, W. Germany

24) [9] J. Paul Getty (US and UK) and Gordon Peter Getty (US), $3.8B ($7.0B), inheritance, oil wealth, investments
25) [10] Mary Idema Pew and family, $3.8B ($7.0B), Steelcase Inc., real estate, Michigan, US
26) [11] Warren Buffett, $3.8B ($7.0B), Berkshire Hathaway, Nebraska, US

* * * * * * * *

A few observations can be made. Forbes did not hesitate to list a family as a single entry on the 1990 list. On later lists, family members would be listed individually. The Mars family, whose wealth came primarily from food products and candy, had greater wealth than Queen Elizabeth II of the United Kingdom. There are no high tech billionaires on the list – neither hardware nor software. Conventional sectors of the economy are represented: retail, oil, real estate, media, publications, communications, and investments. The patriarch of the Walton family is high on the list. WalMart wealth will be represented on the list for the following decades. The Koch brothers are there. Their father, Fred Koch, invented an improved method for refining gasoline. Charles and David inherited their father's business, then expanded it. Warren Buffett is on the list but does not make the top ten.

The next snapshot is nine years later. The year 1999 was at the peak of the tech boom. In this case, I show the top entries of the Forbes wealthiest Americans.

The Forbes list of Wealthiest Americans, 1999 (posted Sept. 1999; inflation factor 1.45):

* * * * * * * *

1) Bill Gates, $85B ($123B), Microsoft (software)
2) Paul Allen, 40B ($58B), Microsoft (software)
3) Warren Buffett, $31B ($45B), Berkshire Hathaway (insurance, investments)
4) Steven Ballmer, $23B ($33.4B), Microsoft (software)
5) Michael Dell, $20B ($29B), Dell computer (computer hardware)

6) Alice Walton, $17B ($24.6B), WalMart
6) Helen Walton, $17B ($24.6B), WalMart
6) Jim Walton, $17B ($24.6B), WalMart
6) John Walton, $17B ($24.6B), WalMart
6) S. Robson Walton, $17B ($24.6B), WalMart
11) Gordon Moore, $15B ($21.7B), Intel (high tech hardware)
12) Larry Ellison, $13B ($18.8B), Oracle (software)
13) Philip Anschlutz, $11B ($16B) oil, railroads, real estate, investments
14) John Kluge, $11B ($16B) DuMont (media, sold DuMont network to Fox)
15) Barbara Cox Anthony, $9.7 ($14B), Cox communications
16) Ann Cox Chambers, 9.7B ($14B), Cox communications
17) Sumner Redstone, $9.4B ($13.6B), Viacom, CBS (media)
18) Jeffrey Bezos, $7.8B ($11.3B), Amazon (internet retail)
19) Ted Turner, $6.9B ($10B), media
20) Rupert Murdoch, $6.8B ($9.9B), publications and media
21) Charles Schwab, $6.8B ($9.9B), finance, discount securities dealer
22) William Hewlett, $6.6B ($9.6B), (high tech hardware)

* * * * * * *

The list looks very different from that of 1990 (comparisons are made with the sub-list of Americans in 1990). The wealthiest person on the 1999 list has ten times more wealth than the wealthiest person in 1990, only nine years earlier. Apart from Warren Buffett, who moved higher in the list by increasing his wealth by a factor of about 6.4, and Michael Dell, who started his own computer (hardware) company making PC clones, the top ten entries are completely dominated by Microsoft and WalMart. Sam Walton died and passed his wealth to his heirs, and each heir is listed individually. If the siblings shared a single listing as a family, their wealth would be $123B, equaling that of Bill Gates. The three Microsoft entries have wealth that adds up to $214B. That's a lot of money, considering they were nowhere near the top ten in 1990. Gordon Moore, who once worked for William Shockley and was a founder of Intel, has a fairly large bankroll of $22B at position 11.

Amazon was a young company, but Jeffrey Bezos makes an appearance at position 18. Charles Schwab, who founded the "Do It Yourself" (DIY) investing house, makes the list at 22. Ironically, many Wall street bankers and hedge fund managers are famously wealthy but I don't see them on the list – or at least not as high as Charles Schwab. It's also interesting to note that the high tech boom of the late 1990s was also known as the "dot-com" boom (followed by the dot-com bust). This is because so much money was invested in internet start-up companies. But no one who derived his/her wealth from the internet is on the list of the top 24 wealthiest Americans.

The next snapshot is 2004, a few years after the tech crash.

The Forbes list of wealthiest Americans, 2004 (posted Sept. 2004; inflation factor 1.28):

* * * * * * *

1) Bill Gates, $48B ($61.4B), Microsoft
2) Warren Buffett, $41B ($52.5B), Berkshire
3) Paul Allen, $20B ($25.6B), Microsoft
4) Alice Walton, $18B ($23.0B), WalMart
4) Helen Walton $18B ($23.0B), WalMart
4) Jim Walton $18B ($23.0B), WalMart
4) John Walton, $18B ($23.0B), WalMart
4) Robson Walton, $18B ($23.0B), WalMart
9) Michael Dell, $14.2B ($17.9B), Dell computers
10) Larry Ellison, $13.7B ($17.5B), Oracle

* * * * * * *

The tech crash was big. For those who were invested in an Exchange Traded Fund (ETF) that tracks Nasdaq (symbol QQQ), each share of their investment reached a high of 109 around March 1, 2000, and by Sept. 1, 2002, the price had fallen to 21. At this time their investment was worth only 19% of its high value. By the middle of 2004, approximately June 1, the price was up to 38 and their investment was worth about a third (35%) of its high value.

Given the magnitude of the tech crash, it's remarkable that the top ten list didn't change more. The Microsoft duo of Gates and Allen lost a lot of their wealth, but their wealth still is high. The fortune of Bill Gates was down to 50% of the value 5 years earlier. That of Paul Allen was down to 44% of the 1999 value. Steve Ballmer dropped out of the top ten. Warren Buffet did very well, even though most of the business world was dragged down. Buffet increased his wealth by $10B in 2004 dollars and moved up to second place. The WalMart siblings also weathered the storm very well. Each of them increased his/her fortune by $1B in 2004 dollars. Adjusted for inflation, the total WalMart fortune was about $115B. In 2004 this is almost double the wealth of Bill Gates; five years earlier their combined wealth equaled that of Gates. Michael Dell, whose company assembles and sells computers, lost about 38% of his wealth and dropped down to the ninth spot. His loss was less, in relative terms, than the losses of Gates and Allen. Finally, Larry Ellison, who derives his wealth from software, increased his fortune and moved up two spots, into the top ten (Ellison was as high as 5 in 2002). It's remarkable that three years after the tech crash, four tech titans (3 software and one hardware) continue to dominate the list of top ten wealthiest Americans. The high tech industry as a whole (hardware, software and internet), did not fare as well as the tycoons at the top of the industry.

The US and global economies weathered the high tech bubble and crash (the crash started in March, 2000), and then survived the real estate / finance bubble and crash (the real estate crash started in 2007, the stock market crash started in September 2008). As discussed in the last chapter, the post-bubble recovery has been led by the high tech industry and, specifically, software. Recall that software alone employs about 1.5% of the US labor force, but software contributes about 7% of the GDP (2015).

The final snapshot of the wealthiest Americans is year 2016 and approximates the present time. I cut off the list at 24, rather than 10, to make a few extra observations.

The Forbes list of wealthiest Americans, 2016 (Forbes, Oct. 2016):

* * * * * * * *

1) Bill Gates, $81B, Microsoft   software
2) Jeff Bezos, $67B, Amazon   internet retail
3) Warren Buffett, $66B, Berkshire   Berkshire Hathaway
4) Mark Zuckerberg, $56B, Facebook   internet
5) Larry Ellison, $49B, Oracle   software
6) Michael Bloomberg, $45B,   media
     Bloomberg LP
7) Charles Koch, $42B,   diversified
7) David Koch, $42B,   diversified
     (5 in 1990, $4.3B each in 2016 $)
9) Larry Page, $39B, Google   internet
10) Sergey Brin, $38B, Google   internet

11) Jim Walton, $36B, WalMart   retail
12) S R Walton, $36B, WalMart   retail
13) Alice Walton, $35B, WalMart   retail
14) S. Adelson, $32B, casinos   gambling
15) Steve Ballmer, $28B, Microsoft   software
16) Jacqueline Mars, $27B, candy   candy
16) John Mars, $27B, candy (1 in
     1990, $23B then in 2016 dollars)
18) Phil Knight, $26B, Nike   shoes (consumer goods)
19) George Soros, $25B, hedge funds   financier
20) Michael Dell, $20B, Dell   computer hardware
Paul Allen, $19B, Microsoft   software

* * * * * * * *

I've now included a category for each entry, such as software or
media. There are notable entries from a new category: those who derive

their wealth from the internet. Amazon.com is a retail company, but its business is built on the internet. Unlike Google and Facebook, Amazon trades in real products and has spent capital on infrastructure that moves tangible goods. But Amazon has no "brick and mortar" stores, at least not yet. Its entire business model is based on the internet.

In fact, four of the ten wealthiest Americans derive their wealth from the internet. Jeff Bezos (Amazon) has vaulted into second place. Mark Z has come from nowhere to reach position 4. This new category has come to dominate the top ten. If one includes the related category of software, six of the top ten derive their wealth from the internet / software business. Let's reflect on this for a moment. In one reliable estimate cited in the last chapter, *software* directly employs about 2.4 million workers, about 1.5% of the work force, and contributes seven percent of the US GDP (2015). According to a separate estimate,[5] the *internet* accounts for 6% US GDP (2015) and directly employs 3.0 million workers, 1.9% of the work force. These figures come from separate studies, and without doubt there is some overlap. One can make the conservative statement that regarding the combined area of software / internet, 3% of the work force (or less) contributes 10% (or more) of the GDP. However, 60% of the top ten wealthiest people in the US derived their wealth from the software / internet sector. This is clearly out of proportion with the distribution of the workforce. We can deduce that software / internet wealth is highly concentrated.

Continuing with the list, Warren Buffet continues to do well. He has increased his wealth by a factor near ten ($7.0B in 1990, when he was at slot 11). Each of the Koch brothers also has increased his fortune by a factor of ten ($4.3B in 1990). The Koch brothers shared the fifth position on the 1990 list. It's interesting that increasing their wealth by a factor of ten, over the course of 26 years, was not enough to hold their position on the list – they dropped down by 2 slots. Three of the Walton siblings continued to increase their wealth but have fallen out of the top ten. In 1990, Forrest Mars Sr. and his family topped the list of wealthiest Americans, with a combined wealth of $23B. In 2016, Jacqueline and John Mars each have $27B but both have dropped out of the top 10 and share the sixteenth slot. Most people would think that they have done quite well. On the other hand, they have fallen out of first place and their current wealth is smaller than that at the top of the list by a factor of three. As a final note, we see hedge fund manager George Soros at the nineteenth slot. Many people believe that hedge fund managers are filthy rich, and they are! But their wealth is dwarfed by the tycoons who got their money from software / internet.

Let's look at another aspect of measures of wealth. What is the historical trend for the wealth gap in the US? Surely there are troves of data that discuss the fraction of wealth owned by a given percentile of the population. In the spirit of the discussions above, I offer a more anecdotal analysis. We've identified some of the wealthiest people in America, at different times and in different eras. In an earlier chapter, I compared the wealth of Mark Z with that of a family of median wealth. The median wealth for a head of household of age about 45 was about $50,000. The comparison with Mark Z gave a ratio of 1 million to one. It likely is a coincidence, but the median family income at this time (a period from 2012 to 2016, with inflation almost zero) was about $55,000 per year. It is difficult to find data for median wealth in earlier times, but values for median income are more readily available. For the sake of a simple analysis, I'll make the approximation that the median wealth of a middle aged head of household is roughly associated with median family income. This assumption might be in error by a factor of two, either larger or smaller. For the simple analysis, the calculation of wealth gap therefore will be accurate within a factor of 4. At the high end of the scale, comparisons will be made with the top one or two people known to be the wealthiest at that time. All figures are adjusted for inflation, using the consumer price inflation index, and are given in 2017 dollars.

* * * * * * * *

1885: At the time of his death in 1885, William Henry Vanderbilt (son of Cornelius) was the wealthiest person in the world. He was the sole heir of Cornelius Vanderbilt. He inherited great wealth and built greater wealth, particularly in railroads. The amount was $231B. In the decade 1880-1890, the median income was about $450 per year. Using an inflation factor of 22.2, the median wealth was about $10,000, one fifth of the median wealth of today. The ratio of the richest person to a person of median wealth was $231B / $10K = 23 million.

*   *   *   *   *

1920: In 1917 Henry Ford was 57 years old. His wealth reached a peak with a value of about $188B. The median family income in the early 1920s was about $1600. With an inflation factor of about 14.4 (from 1922 to 2016), the median wealth was approximately $23,000. The ratio of the richest person to a person of median wealth was $188B / $23K = 8.2 million.

*   *   *   *   *

1974: It's a bit uncertain who was wealthier in 1974, Howard Hughes or the immediate heirs of the Melon fortune. Both fortunes were estimated to be about $1.5B. From the mid-1960s until his death in 1976, Howard Hughes was believed to be the wealthiest person in America. After his death, his estate was estimated to be $1.5B. Accounting for inflation, his fortune was about $7.4B, only 0.15 Zuckr. One can note that his wealth (normalized for inflation) probably was a bit larger back in the late 1960s, $10.4B. The median family income in 1974 was $12,000. Using the same inflation factor, the median income (and wealth) was $59,000. It's noteworthy that, accounting for inflation, the median family income in 1974 was slightly higher than it is today. The ratio of the richest person to a person of median wealth was $7.4B / $59K = 0.12 million.

*   *   *   *   *

2016: From the figures introduced earlier, the wealthiest person in the US is Bill Gates, $81B. The median wealth is about $50,000. The ratio of the richest person to a person of median wealth was $81B / $50K = 1.6 million.

*   *   *   *   *   *   *   *

To summarize, this crude measure of the wealth gap compares the wealth of a person acknowledged to have the greatest wealth in America with the approximate value of wealth of a median household. The ratio of the two is, for the purpose of this model, the wealth gap. The wealth gap has shrunk by a factor of 14 in the last 130 years, going from 23 million in 1885 to 1.6 million in 2016. However, the last 40 years have been very good to the very wealthy. The wealth gap has increased by a factor of 13 from 1975 to 2016.

This final note is a bit of a non sequitur. There is an interesting visual representation of wealth. Reference [6] gives a numerical listing of all the wealth in the world (2015).[6] I've used these figures to create the visual representation in Figure 6. All of the circles are scaled correctly. It's interesting that the greatest wealth is invested in derivatives. Seems a little risky to me. It can be noted that the sources of funds in the derivatives investments are not only wealthy individuals. Pension funds and other public and private (e.g. university) investment funds may be vested in derivatives. It's also interesting to note that the wealth of an extremely wealthy individual, Bill Gates, is clearly visible even on a scale that's large enough to show all the world's wealth.

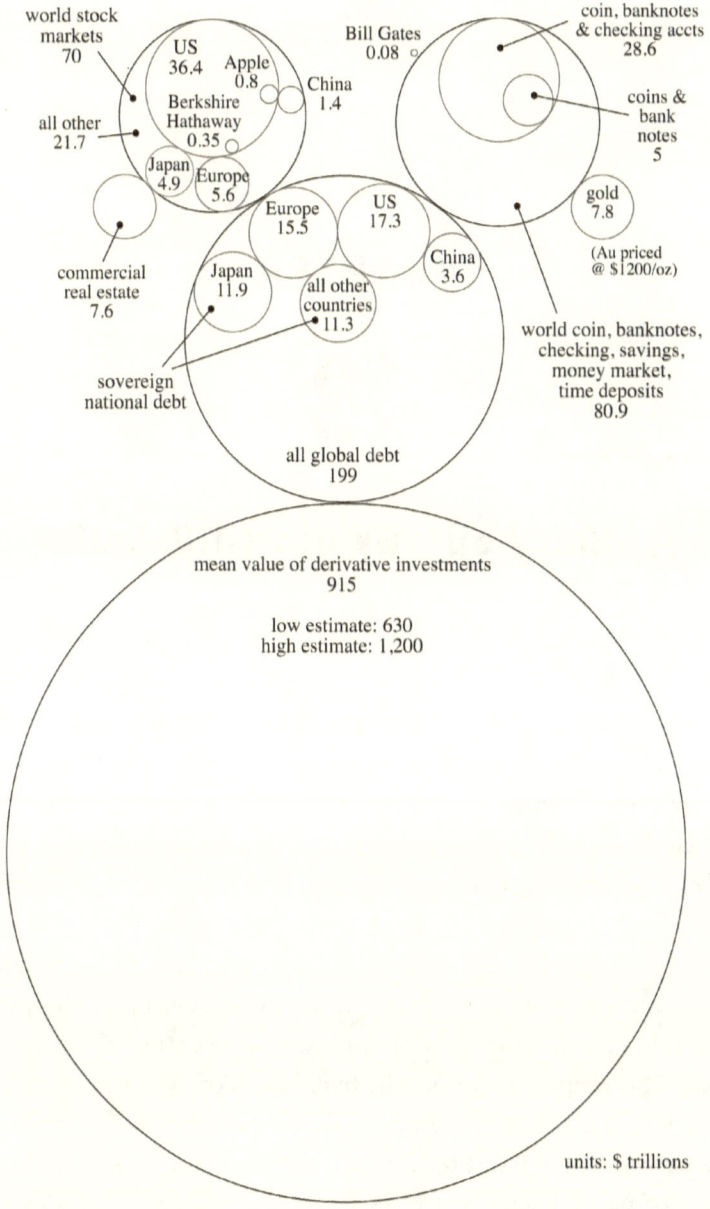

world stock
markets
70

US
36.4 Apple
0.8
Berkshire
Hathaway
0.35

China
1.4

Bill Gates
0.08

coin, banknotes
& checking accts
28.6

coins &
bank
notes
5

all other
21.7

Japan
4.9 Europe
5.6

Europe
15.5

US
17.3

China
3.6

gold
7.8

(Au priced
@ $1200/oz)

commercial
real estate
7.6

Japan
11.9

all other
countries
11.3

world coin, banknotes,
checking, savings,
money market,
time deposits
80.9

sovereign
national debt

all global debt
199

mean value of derivative investments
915

low estimate: 630
high estimate: 1,200

units: $ trillions

Figure 6. All the money in the world.[6]

CHAPTER

13

A Salary Survey of Professions

Software has risen, in just a few decades, to become a significant force in the US and global economies. Distribution of wealth in the software industry shows a tendency towards concentration, and a relatively small number of individuals have achieved extraordinary affluence. With only a few exceptions, the scientists and engineers who made crucial high technology inventions did not achieve significant wealth (recall that in an earlier era, even Thomas Edison had a fortune of only 0.008 Zuckr). More broadly, the scientists who contributed the tests and improvements and whose work developed the physical platform that created the software industry have garnered few financial rewards. This chapter examines the livelihoods of these high technology workers who are further down the ladder. Rather than the top fraction of one percent, the goal is to look at average incomes of researchers in the area of natural science and compare their financial rewards with those in other occupations and professions.

The median family income provides a standard of comparison for wealth and wealth distribution. What is life like for a family that has median family income? In 2016, the median family income was about

$59,039.[1] One typical example of a "median family" is a family with young children and includes a single income provider, the father or mother. It may be equally common for both parents to work but, in a simple scenario, one parent stays home to care for the children. Based on figures from the Bureau of Labor Statistics (BLS) dated May, 2016,[2] the mean annual income of an electrician was $56,650 – pretty close to the family median. Income was a bit lower for a carpenter, $48,340, or for a flight attendant, who earned $51,620. An elementary school teacher, on average, earned very close to the median family income, $59,020. Someone who owns a McDonalds restaurant franchise and works there as the general manager earned about $53,000.

A family with a median income can afford to buy a house with a price in the ballpark of $250K to $300K. Nice homes in this price range are found in areas like Dubuque, Iowa; Columbia, South Carolina; Elmira, New York; Indianapolis, Indiana; and Jackson, Mississippi. These are only a few examples. The streets are pretty safe. Their kids go to good public schools. About 64% of high school students from middle income families enroll in college or university, and about 63% of these students complete a bachelor's degree.[3] In other words, about 40% of students from middle income families achieve a bachelor's degree.

For those who don't start life in the middle class or higher, education can be a key to a higher income and a nicer lifestyle. With a high school degree, seniority with a job in a good trade can give you a median income. When you have a bachelor's degree, there are many careers that will give you a median income or higher. Continuing your education beyond the bachelor's degree by three years, four years or more, can move you to a significantly higher level of income. Achieving a professional degree, such as a law or medical degree, will lead to a high salary profession. A law degree takes 3 years of study. The highest paying positions in law firms require 6 years of service as an associate partner before becoming a highly paid full partner. Medical school requires 3 years of classes and a year of internship. After the conclusion of medical school, a young physician chooses a specialty and serves a residency before reaching the higher pay levels. A residency can last between 3 and 11 years, though the most common residencies are 3 to 5 years. A Ph. D., which is an academic degree, can take 4 to 10 years of study beyond a bachelor's degree. These kinds of positions can be considered as a measuring standard for the upper middle class.

According to the Pew Research Center,[4] the upper middle class in 2014 was defined to have an income between $125.6K to $188.4K, and the upper class was defined to have an income greater than $188.4K (about $200,000 in 2016, adjusted for inflation of 3% per year). These definitions deserve a little more attention. The cost of living varies with location in the US, and the class definitions vary accordingly. For example, the lower bound that defines the entry point of the upper middle class in 2013 (US Census Bureau[5]), had these values for the following listed locations: New York City ($132K); Washington DC ($180K); Boston ($146K); San Francisco ($183K); San Jose ($183K); Memphis ($94K); New Orleans ($92K). With these figures in mind, we can look at what kinds of professions are held by those in the upper middle class.

Using BLS figures from May, 2016, the median salary of a physician in the US who was in general practice was $200,810. This is about 3.4 times the median household income. A physician in general practice went through a lot of training and performs a valuable service. According to the Pew Research Center numbers, the $200,810 salary is approximately equal to the threshold for entering the upper class, though it depends on location. I will use this income as a yardstick for a person who is safely in the upper middle class, and in some locations is in the upper class. I label this as the salary of a United States General Practice physician with a Medical Degree (*USGPMD*), and I define a new salary unit: 1 *USGPMD* = $200,810. I note that the Pew definition for entry into the upper middle class is $125,600 ($133,250 in 2016, adjusted for inflation), which is 0.66 USGPMD in my new units. But earning 0.66 USGPMD does not put you comfortably in the upper middle class. For example, that salary does not put you anywhere near entry to the upper middle class if you live in San Francisco, San Jose, or Washington DC.

Table II

Profession	salary ($) / USGPMD	no. positions
Physician, general practice	$200,810 / 1.0	125,000
Anesthesiologist	269,600 / 1.34	30,190
	340,000 / 1.69 [7]	
Surgeon	252,910 / 1.26	41,190
Orthopedic surgeon	410,000 / 2.04 [7]	
Dentist (general)	173,860 / 0.87	105,620
Lawyer	139,880 / 0.70	619,530
Financial manager	139,720 / 0.70	543,000
Threshold to enter	133,000 / 0.66	
Upper middle class		
Personal financial advisor	123,100 / 0.61	201,850
Pharmacist	120,270 / 0.60	305,510
Optometrist	117,580 / 0.59	36,430
Software developer (systems)	110,590 / 0.55	409,820
Software developer (appl'ns)	104,300 / 0.52	794,000
Securities, financial services	102,260 / 0.51	353,780
Physician assistant	102,090 / 0.51	104,050
Medical physicist	165,930 / 0.83	2,020
Physicist	108,560 / 0.54	20,130

Table 2. Several commonly recognized professions along with
the median income and the number of workers employed.
All data are from 2016,[2] except where noted.

Somewhat different figures are provided by the Bureau of Labor Statistics (BLS) Occupational Outlook Booklet for Physicians and Surgeons (2017 [6]). Practicing primary care physicians (includes general practice, internal medicine and others) received total median annual compensation of $241,273. This is 20% larger than the USGPMD figure as defined above. I will define this as a second reference salary, that of a US Primary Care Medical Doctor; USPCMD = $241,270. An anesthesiologist has median compensation of $443,859, 1.84 USPCMD. A general surgeon has median compensation of $395,456, 1.64 USPCMD. There are two plausible reasons why these compensation figures are higher than those cited above and in Ref. [2]. First, these figures are for total compensation, whereas Ref. [2] gives figures for median salaries. Second, these figures use data from a different source and from year 2017. For the comparative analysis below, I will use the *USGPMD* as the reference salary because I will be comparing salaries for other professions that are provided in the same BLS data base [2].

There are about 125,000 general practice physicians. This is a good profession. It provides a good income, and every physician has many choices for where to live and practice. Other medical specialties pay more. There are 30,000 anesthesiologists and they have a median income of 1.32 USGPMD. As a minor digression, I reiterate that different organizations and web sites report a relatively wide variation for median salary. Money magazine cites a median income of 1.94 USGPMD,[7] and a career information website gives the median income as 1.33 USGPMD.[8] The Occupational Outlook Booklet[6] referenced in the preceding paragraph gives a salary corresponding to 2.38 USGPMD. Thus, the variety of reported salaries show a large range of 1.32 to 2.38 USGPMD.

There are 41,000 surgeons, with a median income of 1.26 USGPMD. According to Money magazine, orthopedic surgeons are especially well paid and have a median income of 2.04 USGPMD. It must be noted that anesthesiologists and surgeons must spend several years in residency before receiving a full salary. After achieving a bachelor's degree and spending 4 years in medical school, an anesthesiologist typically spends 4 years of residency before becoming fully licensed. A surgeon spends an average of 5 years of residency before becoming fully licensed.

Most of us hate going to the dentist, but dentistry is a good profession. After a bachelor's degree, one spends 4 years of professional school to achieve a Doctor of Dental Surgery (DDS) or Doctor of Dental Medicine (DDM) degree and then takes a licensing exam. There are about 105,000 dentists in the US, and the median income is 0.87 USGPMD. Most dentists I've visited describe loving their profession. Plenty of time for golf and lots of freedom to choose where you live and work.

There are several professions that are noteworthy because of the vast numbers of people employed at relatively high salaries. According to BLS, there are about 620,000 lawyers in the US (!!). After a bachelor's degree, one can go to law school full time and receive a Juris Doctor (JD) degree in 3 years. Then one must pass a licensing exam (the bar exam) in order to practice law. There are other requirements as well. One must be able to lie, cheat and steal. The very top lawyers must have the ability to dismember kittens and immolate puppies. And they must have the ability to look themselves in the mirror (to make sure there are no splatters of blood on their clothes) after doing this. Note: there are pills you can take that allow you to look at yourself in the mirror after doing horrendous misdeeds.

There is a large variation in the kinds of law practice that are performed and there are corresponding differences in compensation. Large firms that deal with money (corporate law, financial law) typically require 6 years of service at a junior level. A decent fraction of junior partners are accepted as senior partners. A senior partner position is permanent and carries a very high salary. At the other end, public defenders and lawyers who go into private practice earn smaller salaries. Thus, the median income is not the best gauge for the field of law. Still, the median income of 0.70 USGPMD (which is above the Pew threshold of 0.66 USGPMD) is quite remarkable for a field with 620,000 positions. In 2016 there were about 152 million people employed in the US.[9] This means that more than 1/3 of one percent of all US workers are lawyers. That seems like a lot to me.

Another profession that hires a large number of people is that of a Financial Manager. To be a financial manager, a bachelor's degree in finance, accounting, economics, or business administration is often the minimum education required. Many firms may require 5 years of experience as well. Similar to law, there are other ethical requirements for this kind of job. You must be able to lie like a rug, and show no aversion to stealing the life earnings of a helpless retiree suffering from Alzheimer's disease. Remarkably, there are 540,000 financial manager positions in the US (!!), with a median income of 0.70 USGPMD. This income is still above the 0.66 threshold for entry to the upper middle class. This is remarkable – there are almost as many financial managers as lawyers, and their median salary is just as high. I question whether Financial Management should be classified as a profession because most financial managers I've met have the mental abilities of a carrot. However, the median income justifies the classification.

To summarize, the two professions of law and financial management make up 1.16 million workers (using the term loosely, since many don't really work), about two thirds of one percent of all employed Americans. Their mean incomes are 0.70 USGPMD, safely above the Pew threshold for entry into the upper middle class. Few of these people are billionaires. Still, this is a large group that makes a lot of money. They have a very nice lifestyle, with many choices of where and how to live.

As we continue to discuss the professions on the list, the remaining entries (below Lawyer and Financial Manager) fall below the threshold for entry into the upper middle class. Recall that it's a moving target; one's position in the middle or upper middle class depends on the location where one lives. Pharmacist is a good profession. After reaching a bachelor's degree, a pharmacist can get a Doctor of Pharmacy degree (D. Pharm) in 3 or 4 years. With almost 300,000 positions, there is a wide choice of where to live and where to work. Optometry is similarly a good profession, although there are fewer optometrists in the US, about 33,000. After the bachelor's degree, it typically requires 4 years to achieve an O.D. degree (Doctor of Optometry).

A career that is closely related to financial manager is that of a personal financial advisor. There is almost no official requirement for this position. A first grade education is required. The financial advisor must be able to read, so that he/she can read the statements of the clients who will be cheated. That's a joke. Most have a bachelor's degree in a field related to business or finance. A Certified Financial Advisor must have a bachelor's degree, 3 years experience, and must pass a certification test. There are about 200,000 personal financial advisor positions in the US, with a median income of 0.61 USGPMD. Another career in the field of finance is salesperson for securities and financial services. These people act as agents for the purchase or sale of stocks, bonds and mutual funds. They used to be called stockbrokers. The typical requirement for an entry-level position is a bachelor's degree. There is a fairly wide range of salaries, but the BLS mean salary is 0.51 USGPMD. Remarkably, there are about 350,000 stockbrokers employed in the US. Three professions in the field of finance, Financial manager, Personal Financial advisor and Securities and financial services salesperson, together account for 1.1 million jobs (!), and they all pay quite well.

For a physician's assistant, a bachelor's degree is required. Beyond this, three years of experience in health care and/or a two years long master's degree also are required. One can enter this profession at a young age. With 92,000 positions, there are many choices available. The median income of 0.51 USGPMD provides a decent standard of living.

The Bureau of Labor Statistics Occupation Profiles[2] list a number of professions related to computer software and internet based information processing. Table 2 lists related professions separately, Software developer for applications and for systems software. These jobs typically require a bachelor's degree and pay quite well, in the range 0.52 to 0.55 USGPMD. The number of positions is extraordinary. There are about 1.2 million Software developers in the US. The BLS description for an Applications software developer is: "Develop, create, and modify general computer applications software or specialized utility programs. Analyze user needs and develop software solutions. Design software or customize software for client use with the aim of optimizing operational efficiency." Many of these developers don't actually write code. Indeed, it's noteworthy that there are separate categories for Computer programmers (271,000 positions), Web developers (129,500 positions) and Database administrators (114,000 positions). Not to mention Network and s system administrator (377,000 positions) and Network architect (157,000 positions). The number of well-paid computer related jobs easily surpasses 2.2 million. The not-so-well-paid computer jobs, such as Computer user support specialist ($53,000) adds another million.

Last on the list of Table 2 is Physicist, a career path that I now discuss at greater length. A medical physicist earns a good income. However, there are only 2,020 medical physicists in the US. Furthermore, this specialty is not considered a part of physics Ph. D. programs and therefore I list it separately.

According to BLS statistics, there are 12,190 physicists employed doing research. The position description for this title includes "writing funding applications and publishing articles." While not explicitly stated, researchers that perform these functions have achieved a Ph. D. In addition, there are 7,940 physicists who are employed in teaching positions that also involve performing some research. These positions are dominated by faculty positions at universities that offer Master's or Doctoral degrees. There are some people who hold a Ph. D. in physics and teach in a position that does not involve research, for example at a junior college or a four year liberal arts college. The BLS numbers that I use count only physicists involved in research.[10] The Ph. D. degree in physics, as offered by academic institutions in the US, is a research degree and this discussion concerns the professional prospects for those who do physics research.

Students who pursue the Ph. D. degree in physics are highly motivated and have a focus on a career in research. On average, from the time of entry into graduate school, after the bachelor's degree, it takes an average of 6.3 years to get a Ph. D. It may take further training in the form of postdoctoral research (postdoc) before gaining a professional position. The training time (6.3 to 10 years) is comparable with specialists in medicine, for example an anesthesiologist or surgeon. Still, the median income of a professional physicist is only 0.54 USGPMD. This is less than half that of an anesthesiologist or surgeon, and only marginally above that of a physician's assistant who has 3 years of training beyond the bachelor's degree.

The low pay and low status of the physicist in American society is but one of the problems of this profession. Since we're comparing pay with that of a physician in general practice, let's also compare prospects for employment. The employment rate of a physician is very high. Let's define this carefully. The probability that a physician, with an M.D. degree, will achieve gainful employment in the field of his/her training (medicine, and a specialty within medicine), is extremely high. The employment rate is approximately 100%. From Ref. [6], the number of professionals in the US in the category of "physicians and surgeons" is 708,000 (2016). The following analysis gives a good approximation of the number of job openings each year. I assume that a typical physician leaves undergraduate school at age 22, spends 4 years in medical school, and then spends 5 years in residency. If one therefore starts his/her profession at age 31 and works to 66, we can introduce 35 age categories each with a duration of 1 year. There are 708,000 / 35 = 20,230 physicians and surgeons in each category. Therefore there are approximately 20,230 retirements every year and 20,230 openings to be filled by young doctors entering the work force. According to data from the Association of American Medical Colleges,[11] US medical schools grant 18,950 MD degrees every year. This number is less than the number of openings. A fair statement is that employment of MD degree recipients is approximately 100% and there is even a shortfall of young doctors entering the profession. The shortfall likely is made up by physicians from foreign countries.

The employment prospects for a young physicist are quite different. For a physicist, the probability of getting a job in his/her field of training (research in physics) is only about 20%. This is a shockingly low number. The American Physical Society (APS) releases employment statistics for those who have just received their degrees and entered the work force, and these employment rates are quite high. The trick, of course, is that the APS counts any kind of employment, such as driving for Uber, as employment. The following paragraphs delve into the some of the economic problems of physics research as a profession. These will be of interest to graduate students because they are a focus of some troubling issues. The general reader may wish to skip ahead to the last page of the chapter.

There are no reliable statistics to indicate the number of Ph. D. recipients who find Full Time Employment (FTE) in their field of training. That's because no one cares enough to find out. The professional association for physicists is the American Physical Society, and their primary duty is the dissemination of research results. In other words, they publish scientific journals and organize conferences. They interact with public funding agencies to a minor extent. Here follows an analysis that gives a fairly good estimate of the rate of filling FTE positions. It uses the limited statistics from the APS about employment of recent Ph. D. recipients.[12] The APS polls students who have received a Ph. D. a year after receiving the degree, and asks what kind of employment has been taken. Using these first year employment stats for years 2011 and 2012 (most recently available): 17% took a "*potentially* permanent position" in physics. A "permanent position" refers to a Full Time Employment (FTE) salaried position, and includes tenure track academic positions and probationary positions in government or industrial labs. 51% of respondents took postdoctoral positions in physics. Further analysis requires making some estimates. A generous estimate is that 80% of *potentially* permanent hires succeeded in achieving a permanent position (tenure in an academic institution, or non-probationary permanent status in an industrial or government lab). That implies that 13.6% ended up with permanent positions in physics. Next we consider the postdocs. I estimate that the fraction that achieved a permanent position right out of grad school (13.6%) also can be applied to the postdocs: 13.6% of postdocs eventually achieve permanent positions. That's an additional 0.51 x 0.13 = 6.5%. Therefore, the total portion of Ph. D. recipients achieving a permanent position in physics for that survey is 13.6% + 6.5% = 20.1%.

Here follows a second, independent analysis that uses BLA figures and is similar to the argument used to determine the employment prospects of physicians. The median age of receiving a Ph.D. in physics is 30.5. The average time spent on earning the degree is 6.3 years. I divide the years of a career into segments, each segment being 6 years long; pre-PhD: 25-30; after PhD: 31-36; 37-42; 43-48; 49-54; 55-60; 61-66; then retirement. I divide the 20,130 FTE physicists into the 6 post-Ph.D. time slots. That results in 3,355 FTEs per time slot. In academic year ending in 2015 there were 15,800 grad students enrolled.[13] These students are put into to the pre-PhD, 6-year time slot. From this pre-Ph. D., age 25-30 time slot to the post-Ph. D., age 31-36 time slot, 15,800 is reduced to 3,355. That means that only 21%

of those students make it into the FTE work force. Equivalently stated, the odds of getting a job are 20% The result of this analysis is in good agreement with the earlier estimate of 20.1%.

To summarize, if you are a graduate student in physics, your odds of getting a job in physics are 1 in 5. If you are one of those to get a job, your median earnings will be about half those of a USGPMD. Of course, it must be noted that these statistics refer to any job in physics – the number of good jobs is much smaller. A good job is at a top university where top graduate students will work for you, and where the facilities are very good or excellent. If you have a job in the 95% category of the "not so good" jobs, the grad students are mediocre and the facilities are marginal. As part of your job, you will be expected to build new facilities and recruit top students.

Here's another perspective on the labor force in research physics. There are about 15,800 physics grad students. A very small percentage have full scholarships. Among the others, first year students and some second year students take classes and also work as teaching assistants. It's typical that students from the second or third year and older spend their time doing thesis research and are paid as research assistants. Therefore, the total work force of physicists employed in the category "Research or Research Plus Teaching" (where "Research Plus Teaching" refers to an institution that grants MS and/or Ph. D. degrees) is composed of about 15,800 students and 20,130 FTEs = 35,930 total. It follows that graduate students compose about 44% of the work force. It could be said that 44% of the work is done by students, but that's a tenuous argument. Students work longer hours than FTEs, and FTEs are more efficient in their work. In 2010, median stipends for either teaching or research assistants were $17,500.[14] In 2014 dollars, the stipend was $19,100. This means that the median salary of the group doing 45% of the work was 18% of the median salary of the FTEs, who were doing 55% of the work. The salary ratio is 5.5 to 1. It should be noted that this comparison is made with all FTEs in physics. The professors who direct the students generally make more than the median salary, so the salary comparison between the drone workers and those who direct them would show a ratio larger than 5.5. One also might note that a grad student with a yearly stipend of $19,100 and working 100 hours per week is making much less than the minimum wage.

The purpose of the analysis in the above paragraph is to draw the following conclusion: physics research is funded from the bottom. There is a large population of workers who are paid very low wages and have very small odds of career advancement, and they are called on to do about half the work. This structure is maintained by the professional community of physicists and the physics faculty members at major universities, and it works to the obvious advantage of FTE faculty. I'm not the first physicist to point out that there is an oversupply of recipients of Ph. D. degrees,[15] and I use one final discussion to shed light on the problem of the glut of doctoral degrees. The cost of research involves the cost of labor and the cost of infrastructure amortization and support. The former includes true wages (salary) plus an overhead fee to cover benefits (health insurance, vacation time, retirement benefits). The latter includes an overhead fee to pay for infrastructure and support, sometimes called a facilities fee. For FTE employees, the benefits overhead is about 50%. The facilities fee varies for different kinds of institutions. Industrial labs pay about $400,000 per FTE. At a government lab, the overhead fee is about $250,000. A lab at an academic institution might charge $150,000 overhead. To make a simple illustration, we'll take the FTE overhead fee to be $275,000 per FTE. Then a measure of the cost of doing research for the 55% of the work done by FTEs is roughly 20,130 x ($110,000 x 1.5 + $275,000) = 20,130 x 440,000 = $8.9B per year. Grad students are not subject to facilities overhead, and their benefits overhead rate is about 1.4. So the cost of doing research for the 44% of the work done by grad students is 15,800 x 21,000 x 1.4 = $0.46B. To summarize, roughly half the research staff (44%) is supported at a cost of a twentieth of the other half. If you were at a funding agency that gives out grants and you wanted to increase the number of hours worked on your grant, how would you spend your money? You would tend to give grants that support graduate students. Of course, giving out funding with this preference acts to perpetuate and exacerbate the problem – too many grad students and not enough jobs. This condition, with a large number low-paid graduate students and a large number of young physicists seeking employment, perpetuates the low salary scale. Physics is a small discipline, but it obeys some of the same principles as the broad economy. There are portions of the Phillips curve that apply to Physics. A corollary of the Phillips curve is this: when unemployment is low, employers must compete for fewer workers by raising wages. The converse applies to Physics: the large number of applicants competing for jobs results in low salaries.

How do professional salaries around the world compare with the US? Some salary information for general practice physicians can be found with an internet search.[16] The survey is dated 2015, and probably reflects salaries from 2014. For a better comparison I use the BLS USGPMD salary for 2014 (1 USGPMD = $186,300).

In the UK, the median Medical Doctor salary is 75,500 pounds, slightly lower than the average physician salary of 81,300 pounds ($122,000 USD). We make the estimate 1 UKMD = 0.65 USGPMD. There is a fairly wide geographic variation in Germany. For example, salary rates are significantly higher in Munich and Bavaria than in northern Germany. The average salary for general practice (2014-2015) was 46,000 euros. A similar field called family practice had an average salary of 74,500. The average is 60,250 euro. The exchange rate at the time was about $1.29 per euro, giving an average salary of $77,720, or 1 GermanMD = 0.42 USGPMD. The yearly income of Medical Doctors in India, for family practice or general practice, show significant variation with years of experience. A median value is 430,000 Rupees. A typical exchange rate at the time was 63 Rupees to the dollar, giving a mean salary of $6,825. Therefore, we have 1 IndiaMD = 0.037 USGPMD. A final example is the People's Republic of China. There is a large variation in reported salaries. The parameters for variations include age, years of experience and geographic location. A median salary for "medical practitioners" is quoted as CNY 260,000, which is about $38,000 using the exchange rate for 2014-2015. This corresponds to 1 ChinaMD = 0.20 USGPMD.

The reason for making this last comparison is the following. China and India have large populations and there are many smart people there. If you are a smart person in Asia, and if you are inclined towards math and science, you have a strong motivation to go to the US where much larger salaries are available. Ever since the mid 1980s, about half the Ph.

D. degrees granted in the US have been granted to foreign nationals. This may reflect an awareness among young Americans that science is not a lucrative profession. It also may reflect the trend of foreigners in second and third world countries to seek the higher standard of living that is offered in the US.

What happens to those who do not get a job in physics? What do they do? They may get a job teaching physics at a post-secondary level, such as an institution that grants bachelors or masters degrees. They may get a job doing research in fields other than physics, for example software, engineering, business and finance. If you have a Ph. D. in physics, you are likely to be very good at writing software and many physics Ph. D. recipients end up in software firms. This brings us to our final comparison in Table 2. There are 1.2 million software developers, and the profession is growing. The vast majority have bachelor's degrees and earn a salary approximately equal with the salary of a physicist. If you move to software after completing your degree, you will be working for someone with a bachelor's or master's degree. You will probably be asking yourself "Was it worth spending 6.3 years getting a Ph. D. in physics, just to end up developing software with a million other people?"

If you are very smart and motivated and like science and math, you may contemplate a career in condensed matter or materials physics. Keep the following considerations in mind. After reaching a Ph. D., you will have a 20% chance of finding employment in this field. If you find employment, your salary will fail to lift you to the upper middle class. Meanwhile, the actors who portray physicists on a popular television show made $1M per episode and $24M per year (2016). They will earn more in 4 episodes (1/4 of one work year) than a real physicist will earn in his/her entire career.

CHAPTER

14

A Hardware Startup Anecdote

Those who choose to earn a Ph. D. in physics have only a small chance of finding employment doing basic or applied research. But how are the prospects for an entrepreneurial career path? I've explained my opinion that venture projects involving hardware inventions face many obstacles that software projects don't encounter. I've had a number of experiences with hardware startups that have led me to believe that investors are not very enthusiastic. I recall one of my episodes with some amusement. Most of the story is a bit too technical for a lay reader, but you will understand the ending even if you pay no attention to the details.

Around the turn of the new century I was called to perform *due diligence* for a small start up company, Astro Idea (not the real name). Their setup was a rented space in a warehouse type building in an industrial part of town. Inside there was a lab space, a lounge area and two small offices. The lounge and office area reminded me of a male dorm suite at some state college.

Their idea was to use a narrow beam of electrons to write bit states in a semiconducting chalcogenide film that coated a metal substrate.

More specifically, they would take the emission source from an electron microscope and use it to create a narrow electron beam. Pairs of electrodes, one pair each for the x and y orientations, would apply an electric field that would deflect the beam so that it would raster along a path. The beam current would be modulated with a digital signal to form a stream of bits where each bit was written with either high (binary 1) or low (binary 0) current. A pulse of high current would heat the local spot and change the state of the film to be amorphous (high resistance). A low current pulse would leave the state as crystalline (low resistance). The field emission beam could be focused to have a diameter much smaller than light, about 30 or 40 nm. Therefore, very high recording densities could be achieved. Of course the chalcogenide film has a fairly high resistivity, so it had to be grown on a metal substrate. Readout would occur by holding the electron emitter at fixed voltage, then monitoring the current as the beam followed along the same path it took while writing. When the beam impinges on a high resistance spot, the current is low. When it impinges on a low resistance spot, the current is high. Recording the current while the beam follows the path results in a binary stream of low and high current that gives the inverse of the binary values stored on the film: A high write current pulse results in a high resistance bit and therefore low readout current. The scheme is quite similar to that used for optical recording discs, with two differences. First, the user can write data to the medium. Second, the recording density would be greater by a factor of a thousand.

The device must be operated in a vacuum, of course, because even a small amount of air (or any gas) would scatter and/or absorb the electron beam. The proof-of-concept experiments were done in a UHV chamber. If they worked, a product would be designed to be a sealed unit with the electron beam source opposite the storage media, with a UHV space between them.

I read the reports of the first two rounds of funding, and the material in these reports was somewhere between shockingly bad and amusing. The head of this small start-up company, Harrison, had no technical experience. I never saw his resume. I was told he had a bachelor's degree in either physics or engineering. When we spoke conversationally, he recounted a number of venture projects he'd worked on over the last ten years. He asked about government jobs and salaries. I told him the typical rates for salaries of staff members with a doctorate and he shook his head, remarking that he's been making twice that amount as an entrepreneur dealing with VCs. During conversations with his team, Harrison never addressed specific facts or scientific issues. He projected himself as the visionary and implied his team was there to work out the details.

International Big Company (IBC) had provided the first round of funding. In a portion of their report that was given to me, their *due diligence* team determined that the concept was plausible and offered storage densities that could be several orders of magnitude larger than existing technology.

JBS provided the second round of funding. A year later, I happened to meet a member of the VC team that worked with JBS and he told me an interesting story. He was present when the JBS due diligence guys visited Astro Idea. They had talked for a couple of hours and the JBS guys were noncommittal at best, highly skeptical at worst. At one point Harrison was trying to explain the concept and he remarked: "It's like this episode on Star Trek, where Scottie pulls out this solid state memory bank and adapts it to generate a hologram ...." At this point one of the JBS guys gets excited and says: "Oh, yeah! I saw that episode!" And that was the turning point of the pitch. JBS agreed to provide round 2 of funding because one of their guys was a Trekkie. Astro Idea was now looking for a third round of funding. JBS was hesitant.

From a purely scientific point of view, the Astro Idea experimental results were completely unconvincing. Conceptually, I was bothered that no one had considered the possibility that the chalcogenide film would trap charge during the write process. In other words, I was worried that not all of the electric current would make it to the metal electrode; some of the electrons would get "trapped" in the film. The trapped charge would generate a local electric field, and the local electric field would deflect the beam. So you could write a line of data on a virgin film. But as you scanned along the next line, the beam would wander a little, according to the bits that were written in the first line. The problem got worse for all the subsequent lines. On a time scale of hours, the trapped electrons would eventually migrate their way to ground (the meal film). So if you examined the film hours later, there would be no sign of local electrostatic fields. But if you tried to read the lines of written bits, there would be no coherent pattern.

To make matters worse, the Astro Idea team was claiming that they had achieved successful writing. But they did not claim to have achieved a successful read process. They were seeking a third round of funding based on showing a successful write process which, they argued, meant that they were half way there. But if you don't have a read process, then how can you prove that your write process was a success? They had removed a sample of media after writing, and had scanned the sample with a scanning tunneling microscope (STM). There was a portion of the sample that had some alternating regions of high and low conductivity, and they claimed this represented the written lines of bits. That was hard for me to believe. For one thing, the alternating regions had a spatial variation of 200 nm rather than 30 nm. Furthermore, the variations were not consistent and the difference of conductivity was pretty small. More important, there were no fiducial marks. There were no identifying features. They could not prove that this portion was the region their electron beam impinged. In fact, they admitted that they found this region by spending hours scanning a variety of portions of the film. I took the sample and mounted it in an STM back at my lab. I spent hours scanning the film and never found anything that looked like the images they produced.

I wrote a report stating that I was not convinced that a write process had been demonstrated. I recommended that they make a sample in which they etch away portions of the film to create identifiable patterns (fiducial marks). These marks, where the film was etched away and the metal electrode was exposed, would have high conductivity. They could mount this sample and then scan their field emission beam at low current and fixed voltage. They could monitor the current and it would rise to a high value when the beam was over a fiducial mark. From this point, they could attempt to write lines of bits. Then the sample would be removed, and the STM examination could proceed by finding each of the fiducial marks and then scanning the vicinity to look for conductivity variations that represented their write process. I gave two copies of the report to Astro Idea. They kept one and sent one to JBS.

Astro Idea refused to try my suggestion. I then wrote a final report that recommended against further funding. I delivered a copy of the report to the CFO in person. We'd had several conversations and he knew I was skeptical, but I wanted to explain the report and answer any questions he had. He accepted the report and remarked that he wasn't surprised. We chatted for a while and he showed me some earlier due diligence reports. These were from academic scientists who provided reports that were rejected by IBC and JBS. I read through two of them and I was appalled. I knew both of the guys. Each had a big reputation and each held an endowed chair at a physics department in a top twenty school. Both reports praised the Astro Idea results. They said that the team was "almost there… the progress has been tremendous…." This was pure nonsense. No independent referee for a journal would have accepted a manuscript based on the data they had. By this time I'd reviewed about 40 grant proposals for different government agencies. There was no chance that an independently reviewed proposal from Astro Idea would receive funding from any government agency. These two guys who wrote due diligence reports either were fools or they were eager to be a part of the scam.

To me, this story is a frightening allegory for the tech boom time of the late 1990s and, in a broader scope, the venture capital paradigm in general. Even today I read editorials and articles that proclaim American entreprenuerism – venture capitalism – to be a highly efficient and successful model that should be emulated. However, this case concerned a marginal idea that had minimal chance of success and a $5M check was written because two guys had a Vulcan mind meld about an old Star Trek episode.

In the more recent past I've had the impression that there is little enthusiasm for funding hardware venture projects.

CHAPTER

15

Hardware Research in Decline

I spent decades of my life either learning physics or being a physicist and performing basic research. I was a mentor to dozens of post-doctoral associates and several young staff scientists. I served as an Associate Editor of a premiere physics journal, and have a continuing position on the Board of Editors of another renowned journal. The last two chapters have described observations that might influence career decisions of young people with an interest in science and technology. This chapter continues that trend and a layperson may find himself/herself lacking interest in the discussion – with the possible exception of the remarks on *quantum computing*, a topic that's received a lot of attention in the lay press.

Young scientists complete an arduous training in order to earn a Ph. D. Many sacrifices are made. A number of these young people will find employment doing research as a career. These people will not be financially rewarded. Perhaps they will find personal rewards in the form of enriching and meaningful experiences. Recent decades have been a golden age for basic research in physical science. The Higgs boson was predicted and then observed. The Cosmic Background Explorer

(COBE) discovered and measured the remnants of the Big Bang. A few years later, other astrophysicists discovered that the expansion of the universe is accelerating. The most sensitive instrument ever imagined, the Laser Interferometer Gravitational-Wave Observatory (LIGO), was built. More than a dozen years later it successfully recorded gravitational waves from the collision of two black holes about a billion light years away. These breakthroughs are in fields that pursue curiosity-based research and the results change the way humans understand the universe.

It's been a different story for condensed matter and materials physics. The inventions of fiber optic, diode lasers and field effect transistors, and the creation of the high speed and broad bandwidth communications / information network were of tremendous value to Bill Gates, Mark Z and numerous others who built software fortunes. These inventions also were of great value to society and to the global economy. But for scientists in the areas of condensed matter and materials physics, these inventions had a different impact: Entire labs were shut down and thousands of jobs were lost.

But physicists are smart and resilient and there have been new discoveries and inventions. Most of these inventions have had marginal impact on society, along with negligible economic value. However, of great importance to scientists, these inventions created a new way to make a living. These scientists created a simple model that begins with the promise of a new and important technology. Society responds by funding research programs devoted to the topic. The research in the programs produces promising results. Every year, progress is reported and that's enough to justify that the program should continue. More research is funded and the process repeats. This goes on for a decade or two and then the programs die out and are replaced by the promise of a new and important technology based on a different topic.

The classic example is High Temperature Superconductivity (High TC Superconductivity, or HTS). This was a tremendous discovery for physicists. HTS has had little impact on society. There has been no value to any economy anywhere, and the history of science will pay marginal attention. But the discovery of HTS changed the way that physicists earn a living. It was a highly successful model for generating funding.

High Temperature Superconductivity came along at the right time.

The late 1980s and early 1990s was the period during which industry decided they didn't need physicists. HTS gave the promise of a wildly different world, which would be achieved when the critical temperature of a superconductor exceeded room temperature. And room temperature superconductivity would happen very soon. Transmission of electricity would be free of losses and the savings would be tremendous. Electric power could be stored in superconducting coils for as long as needed, cheaply and with no loss. A new kind of electronics, superconducting electronics, would be developed and superconducting computers would operate ten times faster. Or a hundred times faster. This was the promise: Physicists really are needed in order to make all these things happen.

That was around 1990 (the discovery of HTS was in 1986). Nearly three decades and several $B in HTS research later and the field has come to nothing. However, that model for getting grant money has continued with incredible success. Condensed Matter and Materials Physics have seen many big font topics that have followed the same path as HTS and provided a lot of funding for marginal research along the way. Here's the formula that's been used for decades: "Semiconductor technology (CMOS) is reaching the end of its successful road. Within a year or two it will fail keep up its stunning record of success. We need a new technology to replace it. That technology will become the new CMOS. It will change the world, just like CMOS did. In fact, it will be a bigger change. And for the coming decades it will be just as successful as CMOS has been for the last 4 decades." Below is a partial list of topics that have served their purpose of receiving streams of funding, but have been of zero economic value and/or no benefit to society:

* * * * *

Molecular electronics: This field was started by the single molecule transistor reported by Henrik Schon. Unfortunately, Schon fabricated his data. He simply made it up.[1]

* * * * *

Carbon Electronics: Carbon research is highly resilient. It has come around three times and I'm sure there will be more. There was zero dimensional carbon (Buckminsterfullerene, or Bucky balls [2]). Then there was one dimensional carbon (carbon nanotubes). Then there was two dimensional carbon (graphene). All of these materials have had the same economic value and the same impact on society: none at all. The discovery of two of these three forms of carbon resulted in a Nobel Prize. The third, carbon nanotubes, was mentioned in the award of the prize for Buckminsterfullerene. It's possible that three dimensional carbon will be the next trendy topic. But three dimensional carbon is just graphite, and it's already used for pencil lead. Perhaps the next topic will be fractal dimensional carbon.

*　*　*　*　*

Spin Electronics: Spintronics was on the rise at the time that HTS was falling, and the field caught many of those who were displaced from superconductivity. Research was revived with the reinvention of magnetic tunnel junctions (MTJs), which were originally invented in 1975. MTJs have had applications in the magnetic recording industry. The economic impact has been somewhat blunted by the rise of semiconductor technology for applications in storage. The health of the magnetic recording industry is failing. Spintronics had made broad promises for new technologies to replace CMOS. Despite research investment of the order of $1B and decades of work, none of the promises has had success beyond niche applications.

*　*　*　*　*

Multiferroics: This subfield of materials science studies materials that exhibit both magnetic and electric order. Such a material might combine ferroelectric, piezoelectric and/or ferromagnetic properties. This topic is very popular in the large field of materials science, and research has been active for two decades or more. There have been no applications that have had any economic impact. Many of the promised applications relate to Spintronics. See above entry.

*　*　*　*　*

Topological Insulators: These materials have no possible applications for real products. Many of the promised applications relate to Spintronics. See above entry.

* * * * *

Nanoscience: Years ago there was a field called surface science. It was the study of atoms and clusters of atoms and molecules on the clean surface of a solid (such as silicon). The name wasn't very engaging so they changed the name to nanoscience. That name has been very successful and has spread to a wide variety of phenomena.

* * * * *

Quantum Computing: As discussed in an earlier chapter, digital information processing is entirely dominated by the von Neumann architecture in which a logical operation is applied to a one bit at a time. This model is remarkable successful. Other models might offer new computing capabilities. Parallel processing is based on the idea of performing logical operations on more than a single bit in each clock cycle. The ultimate parallel processor is a quantum computer. The data are represented by the weakly interacting wavefunctions of N quantum bits (qubits). Each qubit is a 2-level system, meaning that it has two eigenstates that correspond to binary zero (0) and one (1).

Quantum Computing has taken up the banner that HTS dropped during its decline. Quantum Computing is an extremely successful topic for continued research. It combines words, *quantum* and *computing*, that carry high value with funding agencies. It promises an entire revolution for computers and information processing. The field is sufficiently esoteric that researchers have nearly complete protection from accountability. There are two key things to keep in mind.

First, there never will be a true quantum computer. The concept[3] calls for representing information as the values of 2^N complex wavefunction amplitudes, where each of the N wavefunctions is a 2-level system (a qubit). A useful computer requires that N should be a thousand or more. A thousand qubits seems like a small number, but the corresponding system with 2^{1000} wavefunction amplitudes is unimaginably complex. The number 2^{1000} is approximately equal to 10^{300} which is (1 googol)^3, that is, one googol cubed. Let's make it easier for the quantum computer and require only 260 qubits. Since $2^{3.16} = 10$, the number of wavefunction amplitudes is $2^{260} = 10^{82}$. How big is this number? It's much larger than the number of protons and neutrons in the known universe[4]!! One can expect problems with a system this complex. Problems arise because qubits are invariably subjected to noise and random unwanted interactions, and the gates that operate on the qubits cannot be perfect. The suppression of these problems is addressed by a process called error correction. Quantum Computer theorists have devised a threshold theorem[5] and concluded that if the error per qubit per gate is below a certain value (around 10^{-6} to 10^{-4}), then computation is feasible. Conveniently, these theorists compute a tantalizing error rate. It's just the right size to permit endless arguments. However, these calculations ignore noise, gate errors and unwanted interactions between gates. In other words, they ignore the problems that are of the greatest concern. Therefore, the theory of error correction, and the viability of performing useful computations, remains controversial. The idea for quantum computing dates to 1993[6,7]. Thus, after 24 years (in 2017) there is not yet theoretical proof that a quantum computer is feasible. There have been some experiments that have claimed to show operation of a small number of qubits, such as 4 or 8, for limited operations.

Second, on some future day there may be a machine that will perform algorithms using gates and qubits, but it will have very small impact. In theory, a quantum computer can perform two tasks better than your laptop. It can find the factors of a given number, and it can calculate prime numbers. These functions might be used in cryptography. Then again, there will be improved inexpensive conventional cryptographic algorithms by the time a quantum calculator might come to existence.

For any of the topics above, the key thing is this: A skeptic must *not* ask about the progress being made or the nature of the issues. Those in the field will respond that "only experts can understand." Instead, the skeptic should ask a few simple questions: (1) How long has it been since research on the topic began? (2) How much money has been spent on research so far? (3) What is the dollar amount of product sales that directly incorporate results of this research? If the answers are 10 years or more; $100M or more; and $0; then it's obvious that the topic has run its course and one must ask if it deserves continued government funding.

CHAPTER

16

Conclusion

In the course of US history, there have been several new and far-reaching technologies that disrupted the status quo and had enormous impact on business. Also there have been individuals who accumulated great wealth. In several cases, one exceptionally wealthy person rose to this position by dominating a new industry. Carnegie dominated steel, Vanderbilt dominated railroads, and Rockefeller dominated oil. All these industries involved a physical product. The product must be produced, packaged and physically moved. Steel and oil require raw materials. Iron must be mined and crude petroleum must be pumped from natural deposits. Steel is then produced in factories and gasoline or kerosene is processed in refineries.

Information technology is a recent example of a truly revolutionary field that has had a pervasive effect on the American way of life and a tremendous impact on commerce and business. The physical platform for the technology came from a few inventions by physicists, materials scientists, and electrical engineers. The companies that controlled these inventions failed to foresee the enormous economic potential that the platform could provide. New companies, typically dominated by one or two individuals, came forward and developed products and services that used the platform and were valued by consumers. These individuals recognized the crucial importance of software and, later, the internet. Unlike the historical examples above, the information technology revolution has been so large that no single person has been dominant. In 2016, six of the ten wealthiest Americans derived his wealth from this field.

Information technology uses a physical platform, but IT commerce does not involve a physical product. Software is composed of bits. Software manipulates information, and the information is composed of bits. The bits are virtually free of charge. They can be stored on a computer or personal digital device. They can be stored in data centers that are operated as part of IT commerce. Bits don't use raw material and are not manufactured. Duplication of bits is nearly instantaneous and often is free of charge.

How big is the IT revolution? Consider five of the most popular companies: Apple, Facebook, Google (Alphabet), Microsoft and Amazon. As of May, 2017, the market capitalization of these five companies is $2.9T (May, 2017). The total market capitalization for all US stocks (October, 2016) is $23.8T.[1] Therefore, the 5 largest IT companies (the Big 5) represent 12% of the entire US market capitalization of publicly held companies.[2] This is quite an astounding fact. There are 4,000 companies actively traded on a major stock exchange. One tenth of one percent of these companies holds a value of 12% of the market capitalization of all companies combined.

The scientists whose inventions enabled the creation of the physical platform that supports IT were very smart and dedicated. They worked hard and persevered. They received bonuses and they were given plaques that thanked them for their work. There are many middle managers in the Big 5 that received millions or tens of millions of dollars in compensation. The principal owners received tens of billions of dollars. Who got the better deal? Among the scientists who invented the hardware, there were a few who were smart enough to take an entrepreneurial role. Several of the founders of Intel, for example Gerald Moore and Robert Noyce, were rewarded as entrepreneurs. But even their rewards pale in comparison with the financial gains of the founders of the Big 5.

The present time (2017) represents halcyon days for software and internet technologies. What about the future? The future, for at least a decade or two, looks the same as the present. There are barriers to hardware development. It requires large scale capital investment in physical resources like laboratories and manufacturing. Also there are barriers to invention and innovation. Inventors have no rights to their work and receive marginal rewards for success. There are no barriers for software development. There is minimal capital investment for resources. There are few barriers to innovation and invention. As the software industry has grown into an empire, the emperors have imposed protective measures for their intellectual property. Employment at these companies can be restrictive in some ways. It's also true that they reward their best employees very well. Furthermore, there is a path for individual entrepreneurs to create ideas and pursue them to a successful resolution.

The logical thread of this short book can be summarized as follows. Several areas of basic physical science research in the 1960s and 70s, those of optics and semiconductor devices, produced very "successful" results. The research resulted in an entirely new technology comprising a new physical platform with revolutionary capabilities - digital information processing speed, capacity and economy of scale; and information transmission with unimaginable bandwidth. The consequences of the success included creation of a new sector of the world economy (information technology) and realization of enormous profits for the individuals and for the software, internet and social media companies that created ways to use the platform. The consequences for basic research and for the hardware technology companies that built the platform were the opposite. The benefit to hardware technology companies was modest growth, at best. A few of the inventors achieved some wealth, though the amounts are negligible compared with the wealth of software titans. The consequences for basic research in these areas have been disastrous. The inventions were so successful that, in many ways, research in these fields came to a virtual end. The best corporate basic research labs in America shut down and they never reopened. A generation of scientists lost jobs, and the jobs never came back. Several decades later, the unemployment rate for scientists with doctoral degrees (with employment defined as doing research in physics) is abysmal. The research that continues in these areas, as well as in related fields, is greatly diminished and mostly inconsequential.

For students, if you are very smart and motivated and like science and math, you may contemplate a career in the Science, Technology, Engineering and Math (STEM) fields. Give consideration to some of the insights offered in this book. Careers in the natural sciences require many years of training. Professional positions are few, highly competitive and the salaries are low. The prospects for finding or creating an alternative, entrepreneurial career path are quite slim. Careers in software offer a remarkably large and growing number of available positions, and the salaries are very good. It is more difficult to break away and create an independent startup today than it was a few decades ago. If that's your dream, there is some chance for success in software.

Index

References and Notes

Chapter 2

1   Time Magazine, Chris Taylor, Reuters, June 17, 2015 [http://time.com/money/3925308/rich-families-lose-wealth/].

2   http://www.newsmax.com/Finance/StreetTalk/family-wealth-heir-children/2014/06/25/id/579236/

Chapter 3

1   The patent application process has not changed much over the last 30 years. A minor change was introduced in 1995 when the PTO began accepting provisional applications. The provisional application establishes a filing date and grants the inventor a year before the formal (non-provisional) application must be filed.

2   Approximately 75% of IP attorneys are male. http://www.skgf.com/uploads/1455/doc/IP Boutiques Still Among Worst For Female Attorneys (Longsworth).pdf

3   Pants that convert to shorts are not a recent invention. The original patent dates to the 18th century.

4   Almost never. There are rare exceptions and my windfall was one of them.

Chapter 4

1   http://www.pbs.org/wgbh/nova/lostsub/hist1580.html

2   http://patentpending.blogs.com/patent_pending_blog/2005/05/us_navy_submari.html

3   http://www.public.navy.mil/subfor/underseawarfaremagazine/Issues/Archives/issue_16/simonlake.html

Chapter 5

1   T. R. Reid, "The Chip: How Two Americans Invented the Microchip and Launched a Revolution," (Random House Publishing Group, New York; 1985, 2001); approximately p. 223.

2   US Patent 2,612,994, issued October 7, 1952.

3   http://www.smithsonianmag.com/innovation/history-bar-code-180956704/

4   Attorneys familiar with the case estimated that the cereal company could have licensed the rights for $15,000, but instead chose to spend $150,000 for the cost of (successful) litigation.

5   http://www.nytimes.com/2012/12/13/business/n-joseph-woodland-inven
     tor-of-the-bar-code-dies-at-91.html

Chapter 7

1   A transmission line is a generic concept that describes a pathway that carries
     waves.

2   Look up the *Shannon Theorem* for a more precise definition of BW for digital
     transmission.

3   A rough estimate for the bandwidth is given by the carrier frequency. A
     red diode laser has wavelength of 650 nm. The carrier frequency is $f = c
     / \lambda$, where c is the speed of light. Using λ = 650 nm gives a frequency of
     about 460 THz. With consideration of some details, a better estimate for
     the bandwidth is roughly 100 THz. A good discussion of the BW of copper
     transmission lines and optic fiber can be found in https://www.quora.com/
     What-determines-the-bandwidth-of-optical-fiber-versus-copper-wire. See
     the post by Steve Byrnes. A discussion of the theoretical maximum BW that
     optic fiber can achieve can be found at http://physics.stackexchange.com/
     questions/56240/maximum-theoretical-bandwidth-of-fibre-optics. Another
     site for a general discussion of the BW of telecommunications transmission
     lines is http://ethw.org/Telephone_Transmission.

4   Generally speaking, a transducer is some device that converts one form of
     energy to another. An example is mechanical energy to electric energy.

5   Jaimin   Bhatt,   et   al.,   "Harold   Horace   Hopkins: A   Short
     Biography,"   BJU   International   vol   106,   1425-1430   (2010);   doi:
     10.1111/j.1464-410X.2010.09717,09731.x.

6   Donald Keck and Peter Schultz, "Method of Producing Optical Waveguide
     Fibers," US Patent 3,711,262 (1973).

7   Theodore Maiman and the first ruby laser: https://www.aps.org/programs/
     outreach/history/historicsites/maiman.cfm

8   A concise history of the light emitting diode (LED) can be found at http://
     www.historyoflighting.net/light-bulb-history/history-of-led/

9   Robert N. Hall, "Stimulated emission semiconductor devices," filed October
     24, 1962, granted as US Patent no. 3,245,002; issued on April 5, 1966.

Chapter 8

1   Personal communication from Prof. Dr. Gottfried Landwehr.

2   T. R. Reid, "The Chip: How Two Americans Invented the Microchip
     and Launched a Revolution," (Random House Publishing Group, New
     York; 1985, 2001). See chapters 1 [approx. page 10] and 4. The traitorous 8
     left Shockley semiconductor to start Fairchild Semiconductor. When each
     member of the traitorous 8 sold his founding shares of stock back to the

company, the price was $250,000. The original value had been $500, so the profit represented an increase of a factor of 500.

3   Robert N. Noyce, "Semiconductor device-and-lead structure," US patent 2981877 A, issued April 25, 1961 (filed July 30, 1959).

4   Kilby wrote a patent application on the broader idea of integration and filed it in February 1964. Note that he filed his application before Noyce, but the Noyce patent was granted three years before that of Kilby. Jack S. Kilby, "Miniaturized electronic circuits," US patent 3138743 A, issued June 23, 1964 (filed Feb. 6, 1959).

5   http://digitalbyte.weebly.com/logic-families.html

6   Andrew Hodges, "Alan Turing: The Enigma," (Hutchinson Publishing Group, 1983).

7   A good explanation of the Turing machine: https://www.cl.cam.ac.uk/projects/raspberrypi/tutorials/turing-machine/one.html

8   This is commonly called the von Neumann architecture.

9   https://er.jsc.nasa.gov/seh/ricetalk.htm See also Ch. 10 for a longer portion of this quotation.

10 Reference [2], T.R. Reid; see chapter 2, approx. page 29.

11 http://www.edn.com/electronics-blogs/edn-moments/4390653/Intel-is-founded--July-18--1968

12 Reference [2], T.R. Reid; see chapter 7, approx. page 29.

13 Beeson, R., Rüegg, H. "New forms of All Transistor Logic" Solid-State Circuits Conference. Digest of Technical Papers. 1962 IEEE International (Volume: V) pp. 10-11.

14 A good description of TTL history: http://www.computerhistory.org/atchm/the-rise-of-ttl-how-fairchild-won-a-battle-but-lost-the-war/

15 Atalla, M. M. et al., "Stabilization of Silicon Surfaces by Thermally Grown Oxides," *Bell System Technical Journal*, Vol. 38 (May 1959), pp. 749-783; Kahng, Dawon, "Electric Field Controlled Semiconductor Device," U. S. Patent No. 3,102,230 (Filed 31 May 31, 1960, issued August 27, 1963). See also http://www.computerhistory.org/siliconengine/metal-oxide-semiconductor-mos-transistor-demonstrated/

16 For FETs in logic circuits one doesn't refer to a current gain because these FETs don't usually involve much current.

17 Operating power for TTL (10 mW) and CMOS (10 nW) gates: http://digital.ni.com/public.nsf/allkb/2D038D3AE1C35011862565A8005C5C63

18 https://www.enterprisetech.com/2014/08/13/oracle-cranks-cores-32-sparc-m7-chip/

19 The CMOS FET is highly efficient yet power is still a problem. Engineers design chips for high functionality and, therefore, use a high density of transistors. The parameter of concern is power density, the power that's

dissipated per unit area of the chip. In the recent past, a typical power density for a central processing unit (CPU) is several thousand watts per square centimeter. This is comparable with the power density of the surface of the engine nozzle of a rocket. It's obvious that the chip must be cooled. Methods include mounting the chip on cooling fins and using a small fan to circulate cool air. There have been some attempts to use miniscule pipes for the flow of cooling water.

20 https://cs.stanford.edu/people/eroberts/courses/soco/projects/neural-networks/History/history1.html

Chapter 9

1   https://www.electronics-notes.com/articles/history/pioneers/ra-reginald-aubrey-fessenden-biography.php
2   Dept. of Commerce, Bureau of the Census, "Census of Telephones, 1922."
3   https://www.infoplease.com/science-health/cellphone-use/cell-phone-subscribers-us-1985a2010
4   250,000 patents behind the cell phone, and Cooper's first cell phone, see: http://www.knowyourmobile.com/nokia/nokia-3310/19848/history-mobile-phones-1973-2008-handsets-made-it-all-happen

Chapter 10

1   Merrill R. Chapman, "In Search of Stupidity: Over 20 Years of High-Tech Marketing Disasters," (APress, 2003; distributed by Springer-Verlag, New York).
2   BASIC was the most common computer programming language in the early era.
3   http://inventors.about.com/od/computersoftware/a/Putting-Microsoft-On-The-Map.htm
4   Windows 3.1 (1992, single license $125); Windows 98 – (PC Magazine, Dec. 1998 $100 single user license); Windows 2000; Windows NT.
5   Refer to: http://www.relativelyinteresting.com/20-years-computing-comparing-1995s-tech-2015s/
6   As an aside, whatever happened to "MySpace"? It was first into the market so Mark Z must have done something right to beat it out.
7   When Edison was awarded the Congressional Gold Medal in 1928, Congress valued his work at about $16B. His personal wealth of $12M (1931) represented about 0.001 of the value of his work. https://www.quora.com/What-was-Thomas-Edisons-net-worth-upon-his-death

Chapter 11

1   Andrew Hodges, "Alan Turing: The Enigma," (Hutchinson Publishing Group, 1983; Penguin Random House, London, UK and Princeton Univ. Press, Princeton, NJ USA, 2014).

2   https://er.jsc.nasa.gov/seh/ricetalk.htm

3   A good site for information: http://www.history.com/news/history-lists/10-things-you-may-not-know-about-the-apollo-program

4   Tom Wolfe, "The Right Stuff," (Picadore, New York, 1979).

5   http://www.armaghplanet.com/blog/apollo-12-1969s-other-moon-landing.html

6   This site has information about all NASA piloted space programs: http://www.thespacereview.com/article/1579/1

7   http://myfirstclasslife.com/15-richest-americans-ever-lived/?singlepage=1

8   http://www.history.com/topics/henry-ford

9   https://www.britannica.com/biography/Andrew-Carnegie

10   http://www.pbs.org/wgbh/americanexperience/features/biography/rockefellers-john/

11   Bits are not entirely ethereal. They must be stored somewhere and there is an associated cost. It turns out they are damn cheap. Consider two means of storage. (1) A personal external hard drive connected to your personal computer. A 1 trillion byte (1 TB) hard drive costs about $100. That represents storage of 10^{13} bits for $100, equivalently 10^{11} bits per dollar. The cost per bit is 10^{-11} dollars, or 10 pico-dollars (1 pico-dollar = 10^{-12} dollar). (2) A data storage center. It is estimated that Google stores 15 exabytes (1 exabyte = 10^6 TB), using 15 data centers. Each data center costs roughly $1B. Therefore, 1 exabyte is stored in each data center at a cost of $1B. That works out to 10^{19} bits / 10^9 dollars = 10^{10} bits per dollar. The cost per bit is 10^{-10} dollars, which is 100 pico-dollars.

12   Tim Burners-Lee: http://webfoundation.org/about/sir-tim-berners-lee/

13   http://techcrunch.com/2012/07/15/four-trends-in-the-public-technology-market/

14   BSA | The Software Alliance, "The $1 Trillion Economic Impact of Software," June, 2016; www.bsa.org/softwareimpact

Chapter 12

1   https://techcrunch.com/2012/07/15/four-trends-in-the-public-technology-market/

2   Bureau of Labor Statistics (BLS), May 2016, Vol. 5 / No. 8.

3   A web search will help you find the "Forbes List" for individual years. Here is a link to the list for the current year (2017): https://www.forbes.com/forbes-400/list/#version:static

4   Howard Hughes inherited his father's company and wealth. His father's company made drill bits for drilling oil wells. Howard expanded his inherited wealth through his company, Hughes Aircraft. Among employees who were aware of the daring and dangerous flying escapades of the owner, the company was known as "Huge Aircrash."

5   https://internetassociation.org/121015econreport/

6   All the wealth in the world; http://www.marketwatch.com/story/this-is-how-much-money-exists-in-the-entire-world-in-one-chart-2015-12-18?dist=tbeforebell

Chapter 13

1   https://www.census.gov/library/publications/2017/demo/p60-259.html

2   US Bureau of Labor Statistics, https://www.bls.gov/oes/current/oes_stru.htm

3   American Council on Education, reported here: https://www.insidehighered.com/news/2015/11/25/study-finds-drop-percentage-low-income-students-enrolling-college; and a report from CNN reported here: http://money.cnn.com/2015/03/25/news/economy/middle-class-kids-college/

4   http://www.pewsocialtrends.org/2015/12/09/the-american-middle-class-is-losing-ground/st_2015-12-09_middle-class-10/

5   http://www.businessinsider.com/what-middle-class-means-in-50-major-us-cities-2015-4

6   https://www.bls.gov/ooh/healthcare/physicians-and-surgeons.htm#tab-5 ; data provided by MGMA DataDive™ Provider Compensation 2015.

7   Alicia Adamczyk, "How much doctors actually make in 2016," April 1, 2016: http://time.com/money/4279561/doctor-compensation-2016/

8   http://www.learnhowtobecome.org/doctor/

9   http://www.dlt.ri.gov/lmi/laus/us/usadj.htm

10 The BLS data for physicists require some interpretation. The goal of Table 2 is to represent physicists who perform research in physical science. Category "19-2012 Physicists" defines the profession as follows: "Conduct research into physical phenomena, develop theories on the basis of observation and experiments, and devise methods to apply physical laws and theories. Excludes `Biochemists and Biophysicists' (19-1021)." Table 2 lists "Medical Physicist" (includes those who work in: offices of Physicians, general medical and surgical hospitals, outpatient and/or specialty medical facilities) separately, for reasons described in the text. Category 19-2012 therefore has 12,160 employed physicists. Category "25-1054 Physics teachers, post-secondary" defines this profession as follows: "Teach courses pertaining to the laws of matter and energy. Includes both teachers primarily engaged in teaching and

those who do a combination of teaching and research." In this category I wish to include those who do a combination of teaching and research. The majority of faculty who spend a substantial fraction of their time performing research are at institutions that offer advanced degrees. First, I exclude teachers at junior colleges, leaving 11,640. Second, the American Institute of Physics publication "Number of Physics Faculty Members," by S. White, R. Ivie and A. Ephraim, *AIP Focus On*; April 2012, gives the proportion of faculty at institutions that grant a Ph. D. or Masters degree, relative to all colleges, universities and technical institutes, as 68.5%. I therefore add 68.5% of the 11,640 faculty at four-year institutions (7,973), who have a mean salary of $98,740. The total number of positions listed in Table 2 is then 12,160 + 7,970 = 20,130.

11 Association of American Medical Colleges, Table B-2: Total Graduates by U.S. Medical School, Sex, and Year: https://www.aamc.org/data/facts/enrollmentgraduate/148670/total-grads-by-school-gender.html

12 Patrick Mulvey and Jack Pold, "Focus on Physics Doctorates Initial Employment," American Institute of Physics, December, 2014.

13 Starr Nicholson and Patrick J. Mulvey, "Focus on Roster of Physics Departments with Enrollment and Degree Data, 2014," American Institute of Physics, September, 2015.

14 American Institute of Physics Trends, Typical Stipends; https://www.aip.org/sites/default/files/statistics/physics-trends/fall10-stipend-firstyr-grad.pdf

15 Prof. J. I. Katz, Washington Univ. St. Louis, posted an eloquent description of the issue on his web site in 2012 (since removed). http://physics.wustl.edu/katz/. See also Jordan Weissmann, http://www.theatlantic.com/business/archive/2013/02/the-phd-bust-americas-awful-market-foryoung-scientists-in-7-charts/273339/, and The Atlantic, February 22, 2013; and Bruce Alberts, Harold Varmus, et al., Proceedings of the National Academy of Sciences 111 (16), 5773-5777 (2014), doi: 10.1073/pnas.1404402111.

16 Examples of physician salaries around the globe: http://www.healthcare-salaries.com/physicians/medical-doctor-salary-md

Chapter 15

1 Eugenie Samuel Reich, "Plastic Fantastic: How the Biggest Fraud in Physics Shook the Scientific World," New York: Palgrave Macmillan, 2009.

2 A Bucky ball is a form of carbon that's named after Buckminster Fuller, who invented the geodesic dome. Each Bucky ball has a geodesic structure with 12 pentagons and 20 hexagons and is hollow inside. The diameter of a C60 Bucky ball is about 1 nm.

3 Michel Dyakonov, arXiv:1210.1782v2 [quant-ph].

4   The solar mass is about 2 x 10^{30} kg. The mass of a proton or neutron is about 2 x10^{-27} kg. Therefore there are approximately 10^{57} protons and neutrons in the sun. The sun is an average sized star. There are about 10^{24} stars in the known universe. That gives the total number of neutrons and protons in the universe to be 10^{81} and that's much less than 10^{82}.

5   D. Aharonov and M. Ben-Or, in: Proc. 29th Annual ACM Symposium on the Theory of Computation, p. 176, New York, ACM Press, (1998); arXiv:quant-ph/9611025; arXiv:quant-ph/9906129.

6   Dan Simon, Université de Montréal, 1993.

7   Peter Shor, arXiv:quant-ph/9508027v2; Jan. 1996.

Chapter 16

1   http://www.businessinsider.com/world-stock-market-capitalizations-2016-11

2   One can ask if the publicly held companies truly represent the total value of American companies. How large is the contribution of privately held companies? A simple argument suggests that privately held companies are less than 20% of the total value. Revenue figures are found more easily than values of company worth. The ten largest public US companies, by revenue, had a total yearly income of $2.69T (2015) [Wikipedia]. The ten largest private US companies, by revenue, had a total yearly income of $0.615T (2015) [http://www.msn.com/en-us/money/companies/the-10-largest-privately-held-companies-in-america/ss-BBiKtaL#image=11]. The income ratio is 4.4 to 1. An upper bound for the contribution of private companies is 18% (this neglects the publicly held companies with incomes lower than no. 10 on the public list but higher than no. 1 on the private list).